THE LITURGY BETRAYED

DENIS CROUAN, S.T.D.

The Liturgy Betrayed

Translated by Marc Sebanc

IGNATIUS PRESS   SAN FRANCISCO

Original French edition:
La Liturgie confisquée:
Lettre ouverte aux évêques et à tous ceux
qui trahissent la liturgie conciliaire
© 1997 Pierre Téqui, Paris

Cover art: *The Murder of St. Thomas Beckett* (detail)
Playfair Book of Hours, French (Rouen), late 15th c.
Victoria and Albert Museum, London, Great Britain
Victoria and Albert Museum, London/Art Resource, New York

Cover design by Roxanne Mei Lum

Contents

Even as they have suppressed Latin in the Mass and have thus shown themselves to be at odds with the decrees of Vatican II, certain clerics have introduced a lifeless, wooden language into their pastoral celebrations of the liturgy. Derisive and contemptuous of the church-going faithful, they now riddle their Masses with a pathetic, pidgin-like jargon, which those who love beauty and seek clarity can never embrace.

CHAPTER ONE

Introduction

"The Tridentine Mass", "the Mass of the ages", "the traditional liturgy", "the Mass of Paul VI", "the Mass of Saint Pius V", "the Latin Mass", "the Gregorian Mass", "the Eucharist", "the Mass with Latin chant"—there are so many ways of referring to one and the same reality: the celebration of the Eucharist, which is to say, the renewal of the Sacrifice of the Cross.

Is this proliferation of terms not indicative of a certain confusion? Is this not proof that we no longer have a very good idea what the Eucharist is and how exactly it ought to be celebrated? Is it possible that we have lost track of the meaning of the liturgy, even while opinions and published works on the liturgy have been growing in number?

In fact, for more than thirty years now the Church in France has been torn apart by a conflict that revolves around the question of the liturgy. The consequences have been nothing short of disastrous, ranging from de-populated parishes to a precipitous decline in priestly vo-cations. These are facts that can no longer be denied.[1]

---

[1] Cf. Meeting of the Bishops of France, Lourdes, 1996.

Who are the adversaries that figure in this conflict?

In order to simplify things, let us say that we are confronted by three groups of antagonists, who are often poorly defined as to makeup and complexion.

The first group consists of the church-going believers who normally frequent our parishes but do not ask themselves any questions about the liturgy, or at least they no longer do so. For reasons that are as different as they are complex, this group accepts the way in which certain parish Masses are celebrated, Masses that are "orchestrated" at every turn in such a way as to adapt the liturgy to the subjective sentiments and expectations of the congregation. These sentiments and expectations, moreover, are often a function of the sociological milieu from which the congregation takes its rise. Numerous studies have shown that the so-called "liturgical training teams", which make bold to modify the structural components of liturgical celebrations without taking into account the directives of the Magisterium,[2] have sprung by and large from this first group.

What can be affirmed without any danger of error is that this group, which constitutes the fabric of our parishes, is less and less a force to be reckoned with, less and less representative in the bosom of the Church. The official statistics on the precipitous decline in religious practice prove this. As for the "liturgical teams" that have sprung from this group, they are less and less coherent in the

---

[2] See John Paul II, *Vicesimus quintus annus*, Apostolic letter marking the promulgation of the conciliar constitution "Sacrosanctum concilium" (December 4, 1988), no. 11.

sense of purpose and direction that they communicate, even though they still retain a kind of "official status" and though they often enjoy a whole range of "logistical supports" whenever they feel the need to arrange meetings or set up refresher courses or reinvent the liturgy. Clearly this amounts to a defeat for the pastoral concerns set in motion by the Council.[3] To be convinced that this is an accurate assessment, all you have to do is travel across our land from north to south or from east to west. The sheer number of churches that are empty, abandoned, and closed, or sometimes even ruinously dilapidated, stands as an eloquent confirmation of it, as are the numerous parishes where Mass is celebrated once a month and even then with poor attendance, while in other instances Mass is celebrated only once a year . . . Allow me to cite an official statistic that was released in 1996 as part of the

---

[3] In a homily dated June 26, 1972, Pope Paul VI said: "Faced with the situation in which the Church finds itself today, we have the feeling that the smoke of Satan has seeped through the cracks and penetrated the People [Temple] of God. It was widely believed that the Council was going to usher in an era of shining brilliance in the history of the Church. Instead we have had storm clouds and shadows, an atmosphere of quest and uncertainty. . . . How could this have happened? An evil power has intervened. Its name is the Devil: that mysterious being to whom Saint Peter alludes in his letter (1 Pet 4)." It is only the expression "the smoke of Satan" that has been remembered from this homily. If, however, a deeper analysis is made of this text, it can be seen that the Pope is highlighting the failure to apply the decrees of the Council in practice. Such being the case, who can be said to be responsible for this failure other than our influential diocesan bureaucracies, inasmuch as they were the ones that were entrusted with the responsibility of applying and putting into practice the decrees of the Council?

preparatory groundwork for Pope John Paul II's trip to
France: for nine dioceses in the west of France, there
were a mere ninety seminarians in formation. With these
kinds of figures it means that in a best-case scenario there
would only be one single priestly ordination per diocese
per year.

Yet, if we look back a few years, it can be seen that
it was the leaders belonging to this first group who uni-
formly imposed "their" pastoral understanding of the liturgy across the board and promised the moon in doing
so. Let us remember that immediately in the wake of
the Council these promoters of the "spirit of the Council"—that infamous "anti-spirit" denounced by Cardinal
Ratzinger—told us that the abandonment of Latin and
Gregorian chant was going to make the celebration of
the liturgy more alive, that "rock masses" would foster
a return of the young people to church, that "liturgical
creativity" was going to make our Sunday gatherings dynamic, that every vestige of splendor in the liturgy needed
to be suppressed, since any suggestion of beauty would
risk offending people's sensibilities by portraying an image of the Church that was altogether too triumphalistic,
and so on. These were the very same leaders who, in spite
of the numerous cautionary notes struck by Paul VI, distorted the image of the renewed liturgy that the Church,
speaking through the voice of the Fathers of the Council,
wanted to bequeath to us. Operating on the principle of
"the more one puts in, the better the result", they pulled
a great number of the faithful who were sincere and well
intentioned into the vortex of their illicit innovations and
harmful experiments. At this point, however, we must,

indeed, have the courage to acknowledge that, as things go today, the implementation of their pastoral projects, which were given more or less official sanction at the time, has led, as is well known, to widespread breakdown and failure. The most spectacular sign of this was perhaps the schism of Archbishop Lefebvre in 1988, although the most significant sign to this day remains the depopulation of our Sunday congregations in consequence of a general process of desacralization.[4] And even today, a few limited successes in the celebration of the liturgy or a local revival here and there or the odd church still filled on some particular occasion should not make us lose sight of the fact that what we are faced with is a total collapse of the religious and liturgical consciousness.

The second group that we must talk about is comprised principally of those faithful who are attached to the ancient forms of our liturgy.

There are many who are tempted to reproach these faithful for never having sought to understand the deeper motivations behind the liturgical renewal desired by the Council or else for confusing the conciliar liturgy with the distortions and caricatures of it that are inflicted on them in all too many parishes.[5] But in their defense it must be said that they have never been given a chance to

---

[4] Cf. John Paul II, *Dominicae Cenae, On the Mystery and Worship of the Eucharist* (February 4, 1980), nos. 8 and 9.

[5] "The current liturgical situation, as is found, for example, in France, is a . . . problem. It is evident that . . . liturgical celebrations are rarely conducted in true conformity with the instructions published by Paul VI", letter of September 11, 1996, addressed by the Holy See to the President of *Pro Liturgia*.

see the conciliar liturgy celebrated in conformity with the current Roman Missal. To this day the liturgy has been plagued by additions, commentaries,[6] idle chatter,[7] and totally unjustified modifications or omissions, which go so far at times as to be utterly inadmissible.[8]

No sooner had the Council been completed than it was impossible to assist at a "normative Mass", that is to say, a liturgical celebration performed exactly as prescribed in the Roman Missal. It must be acknowledged that such a Mass was de facto banned, especially when anyone asked for it to be celebrated in its Latin and Gregorian forms by

---

[6] "The reductive dismantling of a ritual that is already lacklustre is extremely wearisome and demoralizing. In this vein we find, for example, Masses said by the kind of pious celebrant who glosses all the prayers and explains all the gestures: 'Now the priest is about to present to God the bread that has been gotten through the hard work of men: "Blessed are you, Lord, God of all creation. Through your goodness we have this bread to offer . . ."'; 'All together now let us proclaim our faith in Christ who is present in our midst: "Let us proclaim the mystery of faith. . . ."' This sort of thing puts a premium on the type of ritual where a thirst for novelty (calling as it does for a climate of theatrical production and representation) is the predominant theme. This is in stark opposition to the notion of a ritual that has been handed down through time. The latter kind of ritual, that is to say, transmitted ritual, is better understood as a function of collective memory and sensibilities (this does not, however, mean doing away with the need for catechesis of some kind). By way of contrast, ritual that is governed by novelty depends on an apparatus of explanation to reinforce it." Claude Barthe, *Trouvera-t-il encore la foi sur la terre? Une crise de l'Église· Histoire et questions* (Paris: F. X. de Guibert, 1996).

[7] Cf. Cardinal G. Danneels in *30 Jours*; Bishop Defois and Father Charles as cited in *Pro Liturgia*, no. 94; Father Max Thurian in *L'Osservatore Romano*.

[8] Cf. John Paul II, address to a general meeting of the Congregation for Divine Worship and the Discipline of the Sacraments, May 3, 1996.

way of reference to numbers 32 and 116 of the Council's Constitution on the Sacred Liturgy.

Given these conditions, therefore, how could the faithful who belong to this "second group" enjoy any current knowledge of the Roman liturgy as restored by Vatican II? How could they pass judgment on it and appreciate its true worth? How could they love something they have never seen and appropriate it as a gift bestowed by the Church? How could these faithful imagine that the "Mass of the Council", which they are rejecting on the grounds that it is too "modern", is in actual fact the restoration of a pontifical Mass that dates back to the eighth century or that this Mass constitutes, in nearly every detail, the liturgy that the Carthusian monks have already enjoyed for many centuries?

These days the faithful who have formed an attachment to what they imagine to be the liturgical tradition[9] are for the most part those who have never been given the right to assist at a current Mass celebrated in its Latin, Gregorian form, precisely because the order of the day in the wake of the Council (one that held sway at that time in diocesan seminaries no less than in numerous religious houses) can be summed by the following propositions: everything that was done before Vatican II must be forgotten at all costs; the entire spiritual and sacred patrimony that was built up during the centuries that preceded the Council must be gotten rid of. The excess baggage

---

[9] On the liturgical tradition, see the "General Instruction of the Roman Missal" as well as John Paul II's *Motu proprio*, *Ecclesia Dei adflicta*. See also the Letter, *Vicesimus quintus annus*, (December 4, 1988), no. 11.

includes sacred chant, liturgical vestments, altars, processions, incense, and so on.

All we need to do is look at works published in the years 1970–1975 to get some idea of the broad swath of destruction that was visited on our churches at that time and in order to appreciate in some measure the pain that was experienced by thousands of the faithful in the face of blank incomprehension on the part of their pastors. Happily, we are no longer at that stage, and a certain calmness is now noticeable in this respect even though, in all too many places yet, the pain remains keen.

The faithful in this second group are, by their own admission, in the minority.[10] And are they all sure they know how to distinguish between the different rites, between the so-called "Mass of Saint Pius V" and the so-called "Mass of Paul VI"? For many, all it takes for them to believe that they are assisting at an "old Mass" is for the liturgy to be celebrated in Latin and at the high altar, that is to say, with the priest's back to the people. For example, many of the faithful who flock to the Abbey of Fontgombault in the belief that there they are going to find the ancient liturgy in all its completeness are totally unaware that the Benedictine monks have made "adaptations" and are not therefore entirely faithful to the so-called rite "of Saint Pius V" such as it was experienced in the past in the parishes. This example given in passing is a good illustration of the fuzziness that surrounds the question of liturgy in the present day.

---

[10] See *Una Voce*, no. 188 (May-June 1996), 87.

Let us hasten to add, however, that the fact that these faithful are in the minority in no way gives one leave to argue that they should be ignored or that their rights should be held up to ridicule.

Finally, in order to give a complete picture, we must also make it clear that those who are in favor of preserving or re-establishing the ancient liturgy have actually organized themselves into associations that send frequent petitions to the Holy See. To our knowledge, these petitions have neither been approved nor truly been taken into account.[11]

We have come at long last to the third group: What are its true desires and objectives?

We can point out two objectives that serve to distinguish this group from the preceding groups:

1. To see to it that all the faithful can come to know the true "conciliar liturgy" and find it in all parishes, celebrated in its fullness, as required by the official Roman Missal.[12]

2. To see to it that all the faithful who want to can participate in the celebration of the current liturgy in its Latin, Gregorian form in keeping with numbers 36, 116, and 117 of the Council's Constitution on the Sacred Liturgy and Canon 928 of the Code of Canon Law.

---

[11] Cf. Letter of the President of the *Una Voce* federation to the Holy Father and the response of Bishop Rè. See also *La Liturgie trésor de l'Église* (C.I.E.L., October 1995).

[12] "It is my wish, as it is yours, that the liturgy should always be celebrated according to the norms of the Church", Letter of the Apostolic Nuncio to the President of *Pro Liturgia* (September 24, 1996).

These two objectives have a common origin: fidelity to the teaching of the Church in the matter of eucharistic worship.

But if we speak here of "fidelity", is it not right that we should also speak of "infidelity"? Is not the continuing liturgical crisis the consequence of an infidelity to the doctrinal teaching of the Church, to the teaching of Vatican II, to the teaching of successive popes, particularly the popes from John XXIII to John Paul II, who are the "conciliar popes"?

There is, in fact, such a general spirit of infidelity not only in matters pertaining to the liturgy but also in the domains of catechesis and theology that certain intellectuals have seen fit on several occasions to sound an alarm. Has François-Georges Dreyfus not spoken of those French bishops who are against the Pope?[13] Has Marc Dem not asked the bishops: "What have you done with the catechism?"[14] Did the academician André Frossard not consider himself obliged to write a "letter to the bishops" in order to remind them of their duties as pastors and to tell them that their silent collusion with all the doctrinal and disciplinary deviations was becoming intolerable?[15] Has Jean-Claude Didelot not spoken of a "clerocracy" that is at work in the French Church, thus agreeing with Cardinal Ratzinger, who spoke of a "mitred bureaucracy"?[16] And all one has to do is read Pierre Lemaire's *Livre blanc*

---

[13] *Des évêques contre le pape*, (Paris: Grasset, 1985).

[14] Marc Dem, *Évêques français, qu'avez-vous fait du catéchisme?* (La Table Ronde, 1984).

[15] *Le Parti de Dieu: Lettre aux évêques* (Paris: Fayard, 1992).

[16] *Clérocratie dans l'Église de France* (Paris: Fayard, 1991).

sur la famille (White paper on the family)[17] to get some idea of the scope of the fight that the faithful have had to mount against this clerocracy, which has allowed the liturgy to come apart dangerously at the seams and which has, with official support, transformed the catechesis of the 1970s into what amounts to an introduction to the Kamasutra, to judge by the suggestive text and illustrations of certain manuals.[18] Yes, there has been disobedience and infidelity.[19] Whether they like it or not, some of our bishops carry a very large measure of responsibility for this state of affairs.

This, then, is the crisis in a nutshell: in addition to a doctrinal relativism that comes close at times to heresy, we are saddled now with a liturgical no man's land in which everyone has a shot at making up fuzzy pseudo-rituals that are incessantly modified, constantly reinvented, and subject to tediously unnecessary commentaries. We need, in fact, to realize that such celebrations, fraught as they are with uncertainty and taking place as they do without any attempt at notifying the diocesan authorities who are charged with keeping a watchful eye, favor the rise of perverse personalities who foster the belief that the laws governing the liturgy depend merely on their own good

---

[17] *Livre blanc sur la famille* (Paris: Téqui, 1991).

[18] Dem, *Évêques francais*, 143ff.

[19] In the *Nouvel Observateur* of September 19, 1996, Marco Poli, an observer specializing in Vatican affairs, declared, "On regional television in Normandy I saw Bishop Duval blithely railing against Roman authoritarianism." At the time Bishop Duval was the president of the conference of French bishops (source: *L'Homme nouveau* no. 1145 [October 6, 1996]).

will and that doctrinal teaching can be validated only by their own personal assessment of it.

In its wake, this grave crisis has given rise to the growing phenomenon of associations all making certain claims and demands. Some of them demand a return to preconciliar liturgical rites, claiming they have a right to the "traditional liturgy", the "Tridentine Mass", the "Mass of the ages", the "liturgy of Saint Pius V" . . . Others consider it their bounden right to see the actual dictates of the Second Vatican Council being obeyed in the matter of worship. They claim a right to the "restored liturgy" as authorized by Pope Paul VI. It is not important whether this liturgy be celebrated in the vernacular or in Latin, since both of these options are legitimate and the use of the one language rather than the other neither adds nor subtracts anything from the sacramental value of the Eucharist.

However, occupying the middle ground between these two movements can be found large numbers of the faithful who no longer have any real understanding of what is at stake. They think they know what the liturgy is, whereas in truth they no longer have any sort of benchmark that allows them to make a proper judgment on the matter. And because they no longer do have benchmarks, they accept anything (albeit sometimes reluctantly), believing, as they do, in good faith, that whatever the pastor of the parish imposes on them and whatever the "liturgical team or committee" cooks up—or in some cases whatever the bishop of the diocese is prepared to tolerate —conforms to the dictates of the Church.

In all this thick and confusing fog an attempt must be

made nonetheless to look at things clearly. And in order to achieve this clarity of vision, it would be advisable to review three important points:

First, we have the question of legitimate authority in matters of divine worship. Does anyone have the right to introduce changes to the elements of the liturgy? If the answer is "yes", who has the right to do so?

Second, there is the vocabulary used to denominate the liturgy and its ritual elements. What are the implications of certain expressions, and what are the errors they are apt to engender?

Third, there are the legitimate changes that have affected the liturgy in the wake of Vatican II. Have these modifications distorted the liturgy to the point where a whole new eucharistic rite has been created, which is the position held by certain traditionalist movements with an attachment to preconciliar rites?

CHAPTER TWO

Legitimate Authority regarding the Liturgy

Article 22 of the Council's Constitution on the Sacred Liturgy (*Sacrosanctum concilium*) specifies that:

> 1. Regulation of the sacred liturgy depends solely on the authority of the Church, that is, on the Apostolic See and, as laws may determine, on the bishop.
>
> 2. In virtue of power conceded by the law, the regulation of the liturgy within certain defined limits belongs also to various kinds of competent territorial bodies of bishops legitimately established.
>
> 3. Therefore, absolutely no other person, not even a priest, may add, remove, or change anything in the liturgy on his own authority.[1]

The faithful who read this text and see what is happening in certain churches would probably be surprised

---

[1] *The Documents of Vatican II*, trans. Walter M. Abbott, S.J. (Piscataway, N.J.: New Century Publishers, 1966), p. 146. In his apostolic letter for the twenty-fifth anniversary of the Constitution on the Sacred Liturgy, Pope John Paul II makes it clear that: "it is not permitted to anyone, even the priest, or any group, to add, subtract or change anything whatsoever on their own initiative . . ." (*Vicesimus quintus annus* [December 4, 1988], no. 10, in *The Pope Speaks* 34 [September-October 1989]: 226).

to discover that modifications to the liturgy do not come under the jurisdiction of their pastors or a team of liturgy planners but only that of the hierarchical authority of the Church. Even the early Instruction on the Proper Implementation of the Constitution on the Sacred Liturgy (*Inter oecumenici*), dated September 26, 1964, was demonstrably firm on this subject: "Nobody, therefore, is allowed to proceed on his own initiative in this domain, for this would be to the detriment of the liturgy itself, more often than not, and of the reform, which the competent authority has to carry out" (20).

Despite these legislative texts, which are now old and longstanding, the faithful of our parishes have been inured to a reign of the arbitrary, to anarchic decisions, and at times even to a form of authoritarianism that is a throwback to days that were thought to be long past. Many have been wounded and hurt by this turn of events.

It is absolutely illegitimate, therefore, to arrogate to oneself the prerogatives that belong exclusively to the Holy See. Similarly, it is no less illegitimate, on the simple parish level, to substitute one's own authority for the territorial authority that is as a rule exercised by the bishop of the diocese.

But, some will argue, the bishop of the diocese sometimes gives the impression that he is quite willing to approve the things that are done illicitly in our churches regarding the liturgy. Indeed, sometimes the impression is given that these liturgical abuses are the result of directives that have been issued under the official auspices, at the very least, of the bishop's close advisers, if not directly by the bishop himself. When he is informed about these abuses, the bishop never replies. If this is the case, how can the problem be resolved?

A resolution of this problem requires that we should first study what the authority of the bishop of the diocese consists of and precisely what the scope of this authority is.[2]

The official texts of the Church speak of the problem with the greatest of clarity: the bishop is the "moderator" of the liturgy in his own diocese.

What are the implications for him of this role?

According to the Constitution on the Liturgy, according to the decrees promulgated by the Holy See, according to Canon Law and the Ceremonial for Bishops, it is first and foremost the bishop of a diocese and he alone who is charged with monitoring the observance or non-observance of legislation pertaining to the liturgy in the territory of the diocese that has been entrusted to him. It is he whose duty it is to see that it is put into effect, to forbid arbitrary initiatives, and to "root out such abuses"[3] wherever they may arise.[4] Contrary, however, to what is

---

[2] See the final report of the Extraordinary Meeting of the Synod of Bishops on December 7, 1985 (IIB, b, 1).

[3] *Vicesimus quintus annus*, no. 13; *Pope Speaks*, 228.

[4] Several cases of abuse have been pointed out: bishops who tolerate women religious "concelebrating" officially with the priest at the altar; who forbid celebration of the current Mass in Latin; who forbid the use of Gregorian chant; who facilitate general absolution; who forbid younger priests to wear the liturgical vestments that have been prescribed for the celebration of the Eucharist, etc. To be sure, no such laxity appears in official diocesan documents, since these can be forwarded to the Holy See. But it is quite evident in the personal correspondence addressed in the form of an ultimatum to certain priests

all too often believed to be the case, he has no directly legislative power, that is to say, he cannot, on his own authority, make any decision to modify the rituals, nor can he authorize his priests to modify the liturgy.[5]

In accordance with the Council's Constitution, what the bishop can do is call on the help of a diocesan "commission on sacred liturgy", whose prerogatives have been very clearly defined.[6] But this diocesan liturgical commission has no legislative power in its own right. It is not empowered to take any initiative to modify the liturgy or to circulate liturgical training guides that it would proceed to use as a vehicle for imposing new liturgical practices. The commission's sole function is to apply official directives, to facilitate diocesan planning, and, if you will, to do the job of coordination on an interdiocesan level. Its only role consists of taking pains to make sure that the official decisions made by competent authorities regarding the liturgy are faithfully carried out.

The role that each one of the bishops is duty bound to exercise is thus clearly defined. To continue ignoring these directives is to give free rein to an excessive, uncontrolled pastoral zeal that is the first enemy of the lit-

---

who, by their fidelity to the teaching of the Church, refuse to bend to the arbitrary whims of the diocese's pastoral authorities.

[5] There are cases of bishops who, through their official, diocesan bulletins, give excellent directives concerning the liturgy, but who simultaneously, through unofficial information sheets that have been photocopied and distributed to the pastors of parishes, authorize all sorts of suggestions that are not legal. Thus, in the eyes of Rome, the bishop's honor and reputation are preserved intact . . . in terms of appearances, at any rate.

[6] See the instruction *Inter oecumenici* (September 26, 1964), no. 47.

urgy. Too many pastors who have fallen into the habit of changing the liturgy without taking into account the laws that govern its celebration are no longer aware that their actions are more destructive than constructive.[7] In the first place, they are the authors of their own destruction. In reality, liturgical abuses are a phenomenon that reveals a serious shortcoming: that of not being able to interiorize rituals through which personality and social life grow and develop. In the absence of this work of interiorization, which is an educational work of the first importance, certain juvenile—not to say infantile—personalities keep their relationships in a basic state of violence. It is this basic state that explains why celebrants who are the most eager to embrace liturgical modifications are found to have a propensity to engage in "struggles" and "fights" that are none of their business and that they have neither the competence nor the credibility to pursue: the struggle against "exclusivity", the struggle against racism, the struggle for "tolerance",[8] and above all the struggle against any kind of authority, starting with the authority of the Pope and the Roman Curia,[9] as well as that of the Catechism and the Roman Missal . . .

Nor, indeed, should we forget that a celebrant's disen-

---

[7] According to Dom Guy-Marie Oury, in *L'Ami du Clergé* (Langres) 48 (November 26, 1964).

[8] The Christian is not asked to practice tolerance but rather to love his neighbor . . . This puts the question on a whole other level.

[9] On this subject see Bishop Gaillot's instructive remarks right after his audience with Pope John Paul II: the bishop found it necessary to make a clear distinction (an opposition) between the Pope's spirit of openness and the intransigence of the Roman Curia. Machiavelli himself could not have found a more clever subterfuge!

gagement from the liturgy given by the Church usually causes him to seethe with emotional frustrations. These frustrations, moreover, give rise to other desires that have a similar dynamic and which manifest themselves in strident attitudes that may be likened to the behavior of a paranoid personality.

Thus, certain ways of approaching the liturgy are themselves a sign that something is not right: which is to say that it is not, for example, because a person styles himself a director of liturgy that he has the right mind-set actually to be one! In the end, the confrontation with reality—and the liturgy is a reality that forbids any kind of phoniness—always sorts out the true vocations from the false.

CHAPTER THREE

The Vocabulary Used in Reference to the Eucharistic Liturgy

Let us take a few different publications and examine them to see what words are actually employed to refer to the eucharistic liturgy, also known as the Mass.

The Roman Rite

In her official pronouncements, the Church speaks of "the Roman liturgy" or "the Roman rite" to describe the cluster of actions, words, and rituals that constitute the visible face of the eucharistic celebration.

As is intimated by the very name of "the Roman rite", its main outlines were shaped in Rome and then passed on by the living tradition of the Church, so that little by little it became the rite most used in the Church.[1]

This is the rite that the Second Vatican Council set out to restore. What exactly does this "restoration" consist of? Number 21 of *Sacrosanctum concilium*, the Council's Constitution on the Sacred Liturgy, answers this question with a fair degree of precision:

---

[1] See Denis Crouan, *Histoire du Missel romain* (Paris: Téqui, 1988).

> In order that the Christian people may more securely derive an abundance of graces from the sacred liturgy, holy Mother Church desires to undertake with great care a general restoration of the liturgy itself. For the liturgy is made up of unchangeable elements divinely instituted, and elements subject to change. The latter not only may but ought to be changed with the passing of time if features have by chance crept in which are less harmonious with the intimate nature of the liturgy, or if existing elements have grown less functional.
>
> In this restoration, both texts and rites should be drawn up so that they express more clearly the holy things which they signify. Christian people, as far as possible, should be able to understand them with ease and to take part in them fully, actively[2], and as befits a community.

This is a passage of the highest importance, insofar as it makes clear that

— the liturgy includes two parts: an unchangeable core and elements subject to change;

— with the passing of time certain features were introduced that were foreign to the essence of the liturgy;

— the restoration of the Roman rite is not an end in itself but only a means that does not exempt the faithful from the need for personal conversion;

— the rites should express clearly what they signify;

---

[2] The word *actuosa*, which appears in the original Latin text, has been ill-served by the English word "active" or "actively". The *participatio actuosa* desired by Vatican II is an "energetic, spirited participation", not the "furious, bustling participation of the activist". See the Association for Latin Liturgy, *A Voice for All Time* (Bristol, England), 18ff.

— the object of the restoration of the liturgy is to promote the full participation of the faithful in the sacred
action that takes place at the altar.

What is more, in numbers 3 and 4, this same constitution, *Sacrosanctum concilium*, makes it clear that, while the
first concern of the restoration desired by the Church is
the Roman rite, this does not mean that the other rites
being used in the Church (the Eastern rites as well as the
Milanese and Spanish rites, and so on) do not have the
same dignity.

To summarize, therefore, it is evident that, besides the
other recognized liturgical rites, there is one single ''Roman rite'' that the Church uses and that it is this rite
that needs to be restored. We shall see later what kind of
changes will be entailed by this restoration.

''The Mass of Saint Pius V''
or ''The Tridentine Rite''

Those who have not accepted the restoration desired by
Vatican II have fallen back more and more on the ancient forms of the Roman rite. These forms, which were
in use right up to the time of the Council, have been
rechristened as ''the Mass of Saint Pius V'' or also ''the
Tridentine rite'', that is to say, the rite created by Pope
Saint Pius V or that established by the Council of Trent
in the sixteenth century.

At this point, the question that must be answered is
whether a ''Tridentine rite'' or a ''Mass of Saint Pius V''
did in fact ever exist.

We can sift through all the liturgical documents we possess with a fine-tooth comb, but we will never discover the slightest bit of evidence that there was a "Tridentine rite", which some people claim was in common use right up to 1962, that is to say, right up to the time of the Council. Similarly, you will never find a liturgical rite created by Pope Pius V.

On the other hand, it is quite true that it is very easy to find traces of the revision of the Roman Missal made at the request of Pope Saint Pius V. It is quite true that we can refer not only to the Roman Missal but also to the catechism and the breviary arising from this work of revision that was carried out by commissions working at the behest of the Pope. Nevertheless, as far as the liturgy that interests us here is concerned, it is invariably a question of the "Roman Missal", not a so-called "missal of Saint Pius V" or a "Tridentine missal".

That is why we can affirm unequivocally that there is no such thing as a "missal of Saint Pius V" or a "Tridentine rite". We can talk only about the "condition of the Roman Missal" at the time of the Council of Trent, or, if you like, about a correction and reorganization of the Roman liturgy such as were undertaken during the papacy of Pius V.

This is how Cardinal Ratzinger explains it:

> In fact there is no such thing as a Tridentine liturgy, and until 1965 the phrase would have meant nothing to anyone. The Council of Trent did not "make" a liturgy. Strictly speaking, there is no such thing, either, as the Missal of Pius V. The Missal which appeared in 1570 by order of

Pius V differed only in tiny details from the first printed edition of the Roman Missal of about a hundred years earlier. Basically the reform of Pius V was only concerned with eliminating certain late medieval accretions and the various mistakes and misprints which had crept in. Thus, again, it prescribed the Missal of the City of Rome, which had remained largely free of these blemishes, for the whole Church. At the same time it was felt that if the *Missale typicum* printed in Rome were used exclusively, it would help to get rid of the uncertainties which had arisen in the confusion of liturgical movements in the Reformation period, for in this liturgical confusion the distinction between Catholic and Reformed had been widely obscured. This is clear from the fact that the reform explicitly made an exception of those liturgical customs which were more than two hundred years old. In 1614, under Urban VIII, there was already a new edition of the Missal, again including various improvements. In this way each century before and after Pius V left its mark on the Missal. On the one hand, it was subject to a continuous process of purification, and on the other, it continued to grow and develop, but it remained the same book throughout. Hence those who cling to the "Tridentine Missal" have a faulty view of the historical facts. Yet at the same time, the way in which the renewed Missal was presented is open to much criticism. We must say to the "Tridentines" that the Church's liturgy is alive, like the Church herself, and is thus always involved in a process of maturing which exhibits greater and lesser changes.[3]

---

[3] Joseph Ratzinger, *Feast of Faith*, trans. Graham Harrison (San Francisco: Ignatius Press, 1986), 85–86.

The Mass of All Time

Nowadays this expression is used by certain traditionalist movements that would have us believe that the rituals of the Mass had always taken the form by which they were known before Vatican II.

We have seen that this cannot be considered an accurate assessment. The arrangement and organization of the liturgy have undergone considerable variation over the course of the centuries, from the Last Supper right up to the Mass as it was celebrated at the time of the Council and, in between, the Eucharists of the first centuries and the "sacramentaries" that preceded the development of the "*libelli missarum*", followed by the first missals.[4]

Thus the expression "Mass of all time" is deeply deceptive. Its thrust is to lead those of the faithful who are least well-informed, but genuine and sincere in their good faith, to believe that the liturgy was from time immemorial, over the course of centuries, such as it was before the Council; that the Roman Missal fell from heaven ready-made somehow and that Vatican II intervened to break this long, uninterrupted tradition. Thus there is an attempt to promote the belief that the Council was a real betrayal, a serious attack on the authenticity of a liturgical rite alleged to be two thousand years old, a state of affairs that would constitute a sufficient reason to reject categorically the eucharistic liturgy that was restored in the wake of principles decreed by the constitution *Sacrosanctum concilium*.

---

[4] See Denis Crouan, *Histoire du Missel romain*.

The Traditional Roman Rite

This expression is a fairly new one: it is tending to replace expressions such as "the rite of Saint Pius V" or "Tridentine rite". It is used by those who want to promote the belief that the liturgy restored after the Council is no longer "traditional".

As such, the "Roman rite" is recognized, which is in itself a real step forward as compared to those who speak only of the "rite of Saint Pius V"; but the traditionalist groups make a distinction between a Roman rite predating Vatican II, which is traditional, and a Roman rite coming after Vatican II, which is "modern" and hence unacceptable—or scarcely tolerable—even when it turns out that it contains the essential elements of the so-called traditional rite.

What are we to make of this? Did the Council really wish to create a "new rite"? Is the liturgical rite that arose from Vatican II not in the mainstream of the great liturgical tradition of the Church?

We saw earlier that the Second Vatican Council never dreamed of creating a new liturgical rite, a so-called "conciliar rite" or a "Mass of Paul VI" (cf. *Sacrosanctum concilium*, no. 3).

The constitution *Sacrosanctum concilium* is very clear on this point. The work of revising the Roman Missal should be done with two objectives in mind: on the one hand, to preserve the tradition where it is "sound" and, on the other hand, to open up the pathways toward a "legitimate" progress, that is to say, a progress that follows from already existing liturgical forms. This sort of progress, therefore, can occur only in accordance with the principles of an organic development, which is to say, by way of a progressive transformation rather than by abrupt and violent innovation.[5]

There is no excuse, therefore, for teaching or continuing to claim that there exists a "traditional" Roman rite that would be the one in use before the Council and a "modern" or "new" rite created in the wake of Vatican II. When all is said and done, Pope John Paul II has been very clear on this subject:

> The reform of the rites and the liturgical books was undertaken immediately after the promulgation of the constitution *Sacrosanctum Concilium* and was brought to an effective conclusion in a few years, thanks to the considerable and selfless work of a large number of experts and bishops from all parts of the world.
>
> This work was undertaken in accordance with the conciliar principles of fidelity to tradition and openness to legitimate development, and so it is possible to say that the reform of the liturgy is strictly traditional and in accordance with "the ancient usage of the holy fathers".[6]

---

[5] Cf. *Sacrosanctum concilium*, no. 23.

[6] John Paul II, *Vicesimus quintus annus* (December 4, 1988), no. 4; in *The Pope Speaks* 34 (September-October 1989): 223.

CHAPTER FOUR

Is the Liturgy Restored by Vatican II Different from the Liturgy in Use before the Council? If So, in What Way?

It would be useful straight off to make one point clear: the disputes and quarrels that range the partisans of the old liturgy against the partisans of the liturgy restored by the Second Vatican Council have nothing to do with the question of Latin or the question of the celebrant "facing the people" or "with back to the people". Often this is what people have been led to believe, especially in journalistic circles, where reporters are generally very poorly versed in religious affairs but sometimes labor under the illusion that they have the authority to make sweeping statements.[1]

---

[1] To cite just one example among many: during John Paul II's journey to France in 1996 journalists of every stripe could be heard making earnest pronouncements about the imminent demise of the Supreme Pontiff. And then there was the Pope's operation: the journalists were all of them trying to convince us that the Vatican was covering up the Supreme Pontiff's grave illness. At this time, as I write these lines, John Paul II is still alive. Not only that, but he is already giving us his schedule for next year, which is packed full. Curiously enough,

Why does this question have nothing to do with the orientation of the celebrant or whether Latin is being used as the language of the liturgy?

— Simply because the Council never discounted the possibility of celebrating Mass "with back to the people" in order to make use of the old high altars in the sanctuaries of churches. Better and more astounding still: the use of the old high altars is even encouraged so as to avoid a multiplication of "temporary" altars in churches.[2] Any priest who wants to can celebrate "with back to the people" without having to ask the slightest permission from any authority whatsoever.

— Simply because the Council never forbade the use of Latin and Gregorian chant and never made it compulsory to celebrate the Eucharist in the vernacular. Indeed, it is quite the opposite that is required by the Constitution on the Liturgy: ". . . the use of the Latin language *is to be preserved* in the Latin rites. But since the use of the mother tongue . . . may frequently be of great advantage to the people, the limits of its employment *may be* extended."[3] And elsewhere it says: "The Church acknowledges Gregorian chant as proper to the Roman liturgy: therefore, other things being equal,

the journalists have become rather silent now that the Pope's death has been postponed to a later date. See also Gérard Leclerc, *Pourquoi veut-on tuer l'Église* (Paris: Fayard, 1996).

[2] Cf. Bishop Tena, *L'Évêque en sa cathédrale*, in *Documents Episcopat* (Bulletin du secrétariat de la conférence des évêques de France), no. 5 (March 1995).

[3] Vatican II, constitution *Sacrosanctum concilium*, no. 36 (italics added); see also no. 54.

it should be given pride of place in liturgical services."[4] Any priest who wants to can celebrate Mass entirely in Latin without having to ask the slightest permission from any authority whatsoever.

One is very much within one's rights, therefore, to wonder whether the priests who claim to be attuned to the spirit of the Council by forbidding the use of Latin or by erecting temporary altars all over the place (tables, boxes, wooden frames, and so on) have indeed read the official texts and whether the bishops have any intention of putting the principles of those texts into practice.

Since, therefore, it is not the issue of language or music or the way the celebrant faces that separates the "old" from the "new", a person has to wonder about the nature of the rupture between them that has given rise to the quarrels and mutual misunderstandings.

In the final analysis, the antagonism between the old and the new has a threefold origin: in the first place, the minor changes that have affected the liturgy and have been wrongly portrayed as the source of all the current ills; second, the liturgical distortions imposed by celebrants in the name of the Council and brought into widespread use thanks to the silence of the bishops as a body; third, ignorance of an essential principle that is fully in keeping with liturgical tradition.

---

[4] Ibid., nos. 116 and following.

The Changes

The changes that have affected the liturgy have for the most part had a bearing on a collection of secondary elements in the liturgy. All the same, these elements have been visible enough to impart a new image of eucharistic worship.

We mentioned above that the Council intended to restore the liturgy either by abolishing certain rites that, having been added in the course of the ages, were not congruent with the innermost nature of the liturgy itself or by reintroducing practices that had disappeared despite the fact that they represented a true source of richness for divine worship.

What Was Abolished

Before the Council, the Mass was begun with the "prayers at the foot of the altar": when the celebrant reached the three steps leading to the altar, he alternated with his altar boys in reciting the verses of Psalm 42, which was framed by the recitation of the following antiphon: "*Introibo ad altare Dei, ad Deum qui laetificat iuventutem meam*" (I will go to the altar of God, to God my exceeding joy).

After this psalm, the celebrant said the *Confiteor* ("I confess to Almighty God . . ."), which was then repeated by the altar boys. Finally, the celebrant went up to the altar and began his incensing.

During this time, whenever there was a High Mass (a sung Mass celebrated on Sunday), the *Schola cantorum*, totally without reference to what was happening at the altar, sang the *Introit* (Entrance Antiphon) and then moved on to the *Kyrie eleison*.

Prayers said in a low voice; two recitations of the *Confiteor*; an overlap between the choir and the celebrant . . . Any believer with even half-open eyes can see that there were liturgical elements here that were incongruous at the very least. Even if this was the case, however, was it necessary to abolish them? Should there not have been more respect for a tradition that was indeed ancient?

The fact remains that the "prayers at the foot of the altar" were abolished. Why? First, in order not to weigh the liturgy down right from its opening sequence, as soon as it began, and second, because studies have shown us that these prayers were not part of the primitive liturgy. In fact, research into the history of the liturgy sheds no light on the existence of these prayers before the ninth century: customary usage made no such requirement. The priest was merely obliged to gather his thoughts meditatively and say some prayers in the sacristy while he put on his vestments.

It should also be noted that before the Council numerous ancient liturgies (including the liturgies of Milan, Lyons, and Toledo, as well as those of the Carthusians and the Premonstratensians) did not have the "prayers at the foot of the altar", a fact that had apparently never shocked any "traditionalist".[5]

---

[5] Dom Eugène Vandeur, *La Sainte Messe: Notes sur sa liturgie* (Namur: Abbaye de Maredsous, 1946). Note that the "prayers at the foot of the altar" had already been suppressed in the liturgy before Vatican II at funeral Masses and during Lent: these are ancient liturgies which

What did the Council keep? It retained the Entrance Antiphon and put it in its proper place, that is to say, during the celebrant's entrance procession, not during his recitation of private prayers. It retained, moreover, one single recitation of the *Confiteor* on the part of the whole congregation (priest and lay faithful) in acknowledging themselves as sinners.

As for the rest, everything was kept: the *Kyrie*, the *Gloria*, the opening prayer (the Collect), the singing of the Gradual and the *Alleluia*, and so on.

The Offertory, it is true, was changed a fair bit. Let us see in what way.

In the old liturgy, the priest opened the Offertory by turning toward the people and saying: "*Oremus*" (Let us pray) . . . except that there was no prayer to say at this point. This invitation to prayer in the form of "*oremus*" was all that remained of a prayer from a bygone age: for many of the faithful it had become, not an invitation to prayer, but rather the signal allowing them to sit for the duration of the Offertory. For this reason the Council suppressed the "*Oremus*" here, since the rationale for it no longer existed. Instead, they moved it to its legitimate place, which is to say, before the Prayer of the Faithful.

Next, the Offertory rite of the old liturgy continued with the beautiful prayer: "*Suscipe, sancte Pater . . .*". In point of fact, however, this prayer did not, properly speaking, belong to the liturgy. It made its first appearance, it seems, in the prayer book of Charles the Bald. It is there-

---

by and large underwent no great modifications in the course of past centuries.

fore a private prayer that celebrants slowly appropriated for their own use, as is evident in the use of the first person singular.

Then, there came the prayer for the blessing of the water: "*Deus qui humanae . . .*". Why was it also abolished? Simply because the most ancient documents attest to the fact that originally this prayer was not part of the Offertory rite. Rather it was part of the Christmas liturgy, where there is an emphasis on the mystery of the union of the two natures in Jesus Christ within the unity of his Person. It was introduced into Offertory rites only in the eighth century, after the addition of the following formula: "*Per huius aquae et vini mysterium*" (Through the mystery of this water and wine).

The rest of the Offertory was kept almost as it was, with the exception of the brief formula invoking the Holy Spirit ("*Veni, sanctificator . . .*"), which, although it is quite ancient and probably of Gallican origin, was too anticipatory of the invocation of the Holy Spirit that is pronounced at the moment of consecration.

Incensing, which played a role at this point in the old liturgy, is kept in the restored Roman Mass; the celebrant incenses quite simply in silence so as to keep his thoughts focused on the symbolic significance of an action that is sufficient unto itself rather than on formulas to be recited.

Also retained is the washing of the hands (*Lavabo*), although the Council wanted to return to the formula that was used before the eleventh century, which consisted of reciting only the first verse of Psalm 25 and not the whole of this psalm.

Finally, the last prayer of the Offertory ("*Suscipe, sancta*

Trinita . . .") has been abolished as well. The reason for this is simple. Originally this prayer was merely an ecclesiastical custom that had slowly been introduced into the liturgy, beginning in the eleventh century.

Another detail: at the time of Communion, the prayer *"Domine non sum dignus . . ."* (Lord, I am not worthy) is said only once by everyone—priest and faithful—before Communion.

Apart from the prayers at the foot of the altar and the Offertory, the rest of the liturgy has not changed a great deal, even though the final rites (blessing and dismissal of the faithful) have been rearranged.

Therefore, what has occurred has been nothing like a revolution or a rupture with tradition, as is still held by faithful who have been exploited by the excesses of a certain kind of "traditionalist" propaganda that is disseminated through magazines and pamphlets that are sometimes without great doctrinal or historical merit.

At this point, we need to examine certain ritual actions at greater length, for they too have undergone some modifications.

— genuflections: numerous though they were before Vatican II (there were about ten of them), they have only been retained in places where they really express the attitude of adoration that is owed to the Blessed Sacrament. As a general rule, therefore, there are no more than three genuflections that correspond to the adoration of the Body and Blood of Christ at the time of the Consecration/Elevation and at Communion time.

— the kissing of the altar: kissing the altar has become the essential rite of greeting and farewell that the celebrant addresses to the altar. Thus it is done at the beginning and at the end of Mass, and it no longer occurs, as in the past, each time the priest voices a greeting to those who are assisting at Mass. It can be said, therefore, that Vatican II wanted, both in this instance and in other cases, to avoid the risk of sliding into an exaggerated sentimentality.

— the sign of the Cross: in the old liturgy, it was seen as a denotative sign[6] and for this reason was multiplied abundantly. Because of the restorative work of the Council, this gesture has recovered its full significance by becoming once more a true sign of blessing.

Finally, the Council wanted to return to a sense of "noble beauty" instead of settling for "mere extravagance".[7] As well, the Council desired to strip the liturgy of certain "baroque" usages that were of a later vintage, introduced in ages when the Church's prelates copied the worldly customs of the royal court and when subjectivism was so much in the ascendant that the liturgy was made an affair of purely private devotion with all the risks of emotional excess to which this was apt to lead.[8]

---

[6] This explains why, during the Canon (Eucharistic Prayer), the celebrant made nearly twenty signs of the Cross over the chalice and the host!

[7] See *Sacrosanctum concilium*, no. 124.

[8] Extravagance that would explain why in certain socio-political cir-

What Was Introduced

Several elements that the faithful were not accustomed to were introduced into liturgical rites in the wake of Vatican II.

Was this really a matter of "revolutionary" novelties, as is claimed at times by certain people?

— the sprinkling of holy water: the rite of the "*Asperges me*", which in former times had not been associated with the Mass, was expanded and introduced into the eucharistic liturgy as a penitential rite. What we have here, then, is a genuine enrichment of the liturgy.

— the readings from Scripture, of which there were only two in earlier times, now number three at Sunday Mass. They are separated from one another by the singing of the Gradual (or the responsorial psalm) and by the Alleluia (or Tract).

— the Prayer of the Faithful, after the Creed, has been put back into its proper place. Of course, certain formulations of this Prayer of the Faithful can always be criticized as being minimally "faithful" or used for the purpose of socio-political propaganda. But is it the fault of the Prayer of the Faithful or the pastor of the parish if such deviations exist?

----

cles that are full of nostalgic longing for the Ancien Régime there is a stronger attachment to the preconciliar liturgy, which, possessed as it is of a certain splendor, is apt at times to recall the pomp and circumstance of the court at Versailles.

— the Canon (or "Eucharistic Prayer"):[9] it is said audibly. Better still: it can be chanted wholly in Latin, something that devotees of Gregorian chant should rejoice in greatly! Is this a novelty? No: it needs to be underlined first of all that the audible recitation of the Canon was a universal practice before the tenth century. And then there is a rather astonishing aspect to the whispered recitation of the Eucharistic Prayer. The question needs to be asked: What really happened at Mass before the Council? In a great number of parishes, the organ or the harmonium was asked to play very gently and to break off from its music just in time for the elevation, as signalled by a ringing of the bells at the prayer beginning "*Hanc igitur*"; this curious musical practice is fairly good proof in itself that the faithful did indeed desire to hear something. After that, the faithful knew that the Canon had ended when they suddenly heard the celebrant sing out: ". . . *per omnia saecula saeculorum*". This made for a bizarre turn of events, for it meant that the faithful were allowed to hear only the last words of a long prayer, none of which they had been able make out with any clarity.

Thus one cannot help but acknowledge at this point the illogical dimension of this preconciliar practice and so thank Vatican II for having restored a very necessary measure of coherence into the way the Eucharistic Prayer is presented.

---

[9] It should be made clear that the celebrant always has the option of using the first Eucharistic Prayer, which is, for the most part, merely the Roman Canon of the missal that was in use before Vatican II.

— the concluding rites of the Mass have been rearranged in order to help them regain a greater measure of logic.

Let us see how these rites unfolded before the Council: after the last prayer (Postcommunion), the celebrant said "*Dominus vobiscum*", then sang the "*Ite missa est*", using a melody based on that of the *Kyrie* at the beginning of Mass. He repeated a prayer ("*Placeat*"), then blessed those assisting before returning to the side of the altar in order to recite the "last Gospel" (Prologue to the Gospel of Saint John). (This meant that there were always two Gospels at Mass.) Only then was the Mass finished.

It is not necessary to be well-versed in the liturgy to note the basic incoherence of these concluding rites: the faithful are told that they can leave ("*Ite, missa est*"), and yet the celebration of the Mass is continued after this dismissal.

Vatican II wished to put back a bit of order: in the restored Roman Mass, the celebrant says the last prayer, addresses a last greeting to the faithful ("*Dominus vobiscum*"), blesses those assisting, and says the "*Ite missa est*", using one, simple melody,[10] which gives this closing formula the feeling and tone of a command. It is no longer undercut and vitiated by what follows. The Mass is truly finished at this point. In line with this logic, it was never even envisioned that a final hymn should be added.

Is this arrangement of the rites a novelty? Absolutely not: it can already be found in the so-called Missal "of Saint Pius V", to which so many of those who favor the

---

[10] Except for Easter, when the melody is a bit more elaborate on account of the two Alleluias that are added to the customary formula.

preconciliar liturgy hold fast.[11] It is also useful to know that the *"Placeat"* prayer of the old liturgy was initially a prayer that the celebrant said in private when the Mass had ended. Until the sixteenth century, it was not a part of the liturgy. As for the "last Gospel", before the fifteenth century it had been recited by the priest alone, in the sacristy, when he was removing his vestments.

By way of conclusion, the old liturgy that some people want to label as "traditional" . . . is not all that traditional. As we have seen, many of its elements are late additions, the kinds of outgrowths that the Council wished quite legitimately to abolish.

The Distortions

The distortions can be laid at the feet of private individuals. If these distortions are serious, it is because they have changed the liturgical order desired by Vatican II in such a profound fashion that they have caused the faithful to lose sight of the very notion of liturgy, that is to say, the notion of a ritual established by the Church. Among the faithful "there was a loss of the awareness of 'rite', i.e., that there is a prescribed liturgical form and that the liturgy can only be liturgy to the extent that it is beyond the manipulation of those who celebrate it."[12] Exploited as they are by certain pastors on a continual basis, they believe quite wrongly that Vatican II gave permission for

---

[11] See the Roman Missal of 1962, rubric nos. 509 and 510.

[12] Cardinal Ratzinger, *Feast of Faith*, trans. Graham Harrison (San Francisco: Ignatius Press, 1986), 85.

anyone who feels so inspired to invent prayers, poems, hymns, actions, and signs at will.

Is it necessary at this point to catalogue the abuses that can be observed in a majority of parishes? Others have done so, and it does not seem to have changed things much.[13] Let us be content to cite the warning given in April 1980, in the foreword to the instruction *Inaestimabile Donum*: The positive aspects of the liturgical restoration

> cannot suppress concern at the varied and frequent abuses being reported from different parts of the Catholic world: the confusion of roles, especially regarding the priestly ministry and the role of the laity (indiscriminate shared recitation of the Eucharistic Prayer, homilies given by lay people, lay people distributing Communion while the priests refrain from doing so); an increasing loss of the sense of the sacred (abandonment of liturgical vestments, the Eucharist celebrated outside church without real need, lack of reverence and respect for the Blessed Sacrament, etc.); misunderstanding of the ecclesial character of the Liturgy (the use of private texts, the proliferation of unapproved Eucharistic Prayers, the manipulation of the liturgical texts for social and political ends). In these cases we are face to face with a real falsification of the Catholic Liturgy: "One who offers worship to God on the Church's behalf in a way contrary to that which is laid down by the Church with God-given authority and which is customary in the Church is guilty of falsification" (St. Thomas, *Summa Theologiae*, 2–2, q. 93, a. 1).

None of these things can bring good results. The con-

---

[13] André Mignot and Michel de Saint-Pierre, *Les Fumées de Satan* (Paris: La Table Ronde, 1976), 83–135.

sequences are—and cannot fail to be—the impairing of
the unity of Faith and worship in the Church, doctrinal
uncertainty, scandal and bewilderment among the People
of God, and the near inevitability of violent reactions.

The faithful have a right to a true Liturgy, which means
the Liturgy desired and laid down by the Church, which
has in fact indicated where adaptations may be made as
called for by pastoral requirements in different places or
by different groups of people. Undue experimentation,
changes and creativity bewilder the faithful.[14]

Inaestimabile Donum, which has been quoted in part
here, echoes a letter issued by John Paul II in February
1980, in which the Sovereign Pontiff alludes to the serious abuses:

The priest as minister, as celebrant, as the one who presides over the Eucharistic assembly of the faithful, should
have a special sense of the common good of the Church,
which he represents through his ministry, but to which he
must also be subordinate, according to a correct discipline
of faith. He cannot consider himself a "proprietor" who
can make free use of the liturgical text and of the sacred
rite as if it were his own property, in such a way as to
stamp it with his own arbitrary personal style. At times
this latter might seem more effective, and it may better
correspond to subjective piety; nevertheless, objectively
it is always a betrayal of that union which should find its
proper expression in the Sacrament of unity.

Every priest who offers the Holy Sacrifice should recall that during this Sacrifice it is not only he with his

---

[14] Sacred Congregation for the Sacraments and Divine Worship, Instruction concerning Worship of the Eucharistic Mystery, *Inaestimabile
Donum*, April 17, 1980 (Boston: Daughters of St. Paul, 1980).

community that is praying but the whole Church, which
is thus expressing in this Sacrament her spiritual unity,
among other ways by the use of the approved liturgical
text. To call this position "mere insistence on uniformity"
would only show ignorance of the objective requirements
of authentic unity, and would be a symptom of harmful
individualism.

This subordination of the minister, of the celebrant, to
the *Mysterium* which has been entrusted to him by the
Church for the good of the whole People of God, should
also find expression in the observance of the liturgical requirements concerning the celebration of the Holy Sacrifice. These refer for example to dress, and in particular
to the vestments worn by the celebrant. Circumstances
have of course existed and continue to exist in which the
prescriptions do not oblige. We have been greatly moved
when reading books written by priests who had been pris-
oners in extermination camps, with descriptions of Eucharistic celebrations without the above-mentioned rules,
that is to say without an altar and without vestments. But
although in those conditions this was a proof of heroism
and deserved profound admiration, nevertheless in normal
conditions to ignore the liturgical directives can be inter-
preted as a lack of respect towards the Eucharist, dictated
perhaps by individualism or by an absence of a critical
sense concerning current opinions, or by a certain lack of
a spirit of faith.[15]

These two excerpts have been chosen from among
many that show that those in authority have always wanted

---

[15] John Paul II, "On the Mystery and Worship of the Eucharist, *Do-
minicae cenae*", February 24, 1980, art. 12, from *Vatican Council II: More
Post Conciliar Documents*, ed. Austin Flannery, O.P. (Northpoint, N.Y.:
Costello Publishing, 1982), 84–85.

to remind us that often what was done "in the name of the Council" was not in conformity with what the Council had really desired and harmoniously arranged. Nonetheless, it is regrettable that these warnings have not been echoed by diocesan officials. Rather the latter, when informed of certain distortions, have almost always preferred unjustly to blame, not those who are the cause of the scandal, but rather those who are denouncing it. Clearly, falsifying doctrine is a less serious offense than undermining the prestige of a member of the establishment.

Recalling an Essential Principle of Tradition

The most important liturgical principle to have been recalled by the Second Vatican Council's Constitution on the Sacred Liturgy, a principle that is still to this day honored more in the breach than in the observance, is the following: "In liturgical celebrations, whether as a minister or as one of the faithful, each person should perform his role by doing solely and totally what the nature of things and liturgical norms require of him."[16]

What the Council is recalling here is that, in the liturgy, everyone—the faithful no less than ministers—has a particular function to fulfill. Which is to say that anyone who performs a specific liturgical ministry (priest, deacon, choir member) must not encroach upon another function that is not his: the celebrant at the altar is not the liturgical director or the commentator; the congrega-

---

[16] *Sacrosanctum concilium*, no. 28.

tion does not replace the choir, and the choir does not replace the congregation, and so on. The text of the constitution stresses that it is necessary for each person to discover his own vocation and fulfill it exactly, without seeking to play a role of substitution: for whoever fulfills a function for which he is not fitted or prepared, whoever is not in his proper place, inevitably becomes a sanctimonious hypocrite who transforms the liturgy into a display of grotesque buffoonery, into "a shabby spectacle that is not worth going to", as Cardinal Danneels puts it.[17] In the liturgy we should do only what corresponds with what we really are and not do what corresponds to what we would have liked to be or what we imagine we are: if liturgical ritual becomes an instrument that allows certain persons to make up for their shortcomings, it is the liturgy as a whole that runs the risk of becoming for the faithful who participate in it a vehicle for neurotic behavior.[18]

In order for there to be a sound basis to the liturgy, each actor in the liturgy should therefore fulfill his function by respecting two essential aspects: the nature of things, on the one hand, and liturgical norms, on the other. Which is to say that improvisation, arbitrariness, and manifes-

---

[17] See the article that appeared in *Le Figaro* on December 7, 1996.

[18] This is why it is advisable to be extremely prudent in the choice of persons who are in charge of liturgical direction and to avoid calling on exseminarians who did not follow through to the end with their vocation, on religious in civilian dress, on divorced men and women, and on widows and widowers who have not adequately undergone a period of mourning, etc. This is not because people like this, who are often full of good will, should be systematically excluded, but because the liturgy must be guaranteed a healthy role to play.

tations of individualism all turn out to be elements that are no longer acceptable, to the extent that they ruin the harmony of the liturgy: the things of the liturgy are what they are by virtue of the purpose that is given to them by the Church, and not by virtue of what one imagines them to be or what one would like them to be.

We are merely dealing here with an essential balancing principle: in all our actions, but mainly in the liturgy, which is the "action" par excellence, too much rationalization detracts from reality, while an excess of emotion means that it is only the affective dimension that governs in an irrational way our behavior and the choices we make in life.[19] There is thus a point of balance that must be found. This is situated somewhere between hyperrationalism and hyperemotionalism and consists of being totally present in the action that has to be performed.

As a result, the mind (one could even use the word "brain" here) of each participant in the liturgy needs to be applied—or "adapted"—to what he is doing. In the behavior of those who are participants in the liturgy, there should be no perceptible doubt, no hesitation betraying the slightest hint of a wandering mind. This would be the sign of a "false vocation", that is to say, an inability on the part of the person to adapt to the objective that he lays claim to attaining. In the final analysis, it can be said

---

[19] This is where the danger lies in certain hymns of the present day. Their words and harmonies strike an affective chord, generating murky, ambiguous sentiments. In the case of Gregorian chant, on the other hand, the structure of the music conveys sound and accurate sentiments (although even Gregorian chant can be misrepresented and betrayed if it is performed in a preciously sentimental or romantic way).

that every vocation (in the sense of disposition) is sooner or later tested in terms of aptitude and competence. This notion has always been understood as arising quite obviously from the realm of common sense. In popular parlance a person who does a poor job of something he had intended to bring to completion is said to have "missed the mark". Now when a person wants to do a thing for which he has no real aptitude—which can be determined at first glance—the whole situation tends to make him a laughing-stock.[20]

It is in this perspective of "true vocation" that *Sacrosanctum concilium*, the Constitution on the Sacred Liturgy, needs to be read, understood, and applied.

After all, number 28 of the constitution is complemented by number 34: "The rites should be distinguished by a noble simplicity; they should be short, clear, and unencumbered by useless repetitions."

Inasmuch as each person does no more than what he has to do, the repetition of certain prayers, such as found in the Roman liturgy before the Council (especially at a High Mass), is abolished.

What, in point of fact, was the utterly incongruous aspect of the old liturgy?

It must be remembered that the so-called missal of "Saint Pius V" was a "plenary missal", which is to say, it was conceived as a book that allowed the priest to ensure that he could carry out all the liturgical functions by

---

[20] This is the whole problem with celebrants, cantors, and liturgical directors who "theatricalize" the liturgy in order to achieve a sense of security and who, in the final analysis, make fools of themselves. (See certain televised Masses, for example.)

himself. This may have been practical in small parishes where quite often the priest had to do everything himself at the altar. But as soon as the celebrant was assisted by a choir, everything about this arrangement became "nonsensical". What happened, in reality, was that at the altar the celebrant continued to say Mass in a low voice, just as if he were alone: wearing as it were several liturgical hats at once, he personally recited all the prayers that the choir was responsible for singing. In this way it came to be that numerous parts of the celebration were duplicated. This is why, before the Council, the parish "High Mass" had two repetitions of the *Kyrie*, two of the *Gloria*, two Graduals, two instances of the *Alleluia*, two of the *Credo*, two of the *Sanctus*, two of the *Agnus Dei*, three of the *Confiteor*, six of the *Domine, non sum dignus*. What is more, since there was ordinarily an interval between what the priest recited rapidly at the altar and what the choir and the congregation sang more slowly, the liturgical ritual allowed the celebrant and the altar boys to go and sit down while they waited for the singing to be finished.

All of this, it must be stressed, was totally out of keeping with the most venerable and long-standing liturgical traditions, which

— have always avoided repetitions and doublets, and

— have always taken care to distribute roles between different actors, as witnessed by the most ancient liturgical books: sacramentaries, lectionaries, antiphonaries, evangelistaries, and so on.

The question now is to find out why, instead of calling for pastors to respect the present liturgy, some of the faithful have attached themselves to the old liturgy; this is what we are going to try to answer briefly.

CHAPTER FIVE

The Attachment of the Faithful
to the Old Liturgy

If some of the faithful remain attached to the old liturgy
at the present time, it is for many reasons, many of them
complex. What follows are brief sketches of some of these
reasons:

Ignorance of the Principles of Liturgical
Renewal Desired by Vatican II

As things stand, in more than 90 percent of the churches
in France, the liturgy is not celebrated in accordance with
the norms set down by the present Roman Missal. Making
an assertion like this is not meant to be construed as an
unconditionally negative criticism. It is merely to make
a statement of fact that is also conceded by the highest
authorities.[1]

---

[1] "The current liturgical situation, as it presents itself in France,
for example, is another problem. On the one hand, it is rare to see
liturgical celebrations performed in true accordance with the books
published by edict of Paul VI, while, on the other hand, it is clear to
see that there has been a return of sorts to an earlier liturgy. The full
significance of these undeniable facts remains to be seen, although one
day the consequences of this state of affairs will need to be faced."

It must indeed be acknowledged that a veritable armada of diocesan bureaucrats, self-proclaimed "liturgical coordinators", have invaded the liturgical life of parishes. Here, in place of the beautiful liturgy restored by the Council (which can be seen celebrated correctly in monasteries like Solesmes, Kergonan, Saint-Wandrille, and other places), they have substituted shoddy, liturgical rubbish, which is interchangeable[2] in its banality and leaves no lasting impression in the minds and hearts of the faithful. In the majority of our churches, little "witness stories" and little songs sung by little voices make a vain attempt to bring some life to little Masses celebrated at little altars for little congregations. The liturgy has become "little", that is to say, pathetically ridiculous, incapable of arousing the interest and support of an average member of the faithful who has been properly catechized. The liturgy has become precisely the opposite of what the Council wanted it to become: simple, to be sure, but simple in the terms laid down in the Constitution on the Liturgy, "noble", "dignified", "harmonious", "beautiful", "radiant", and capable of being a reflection of the liturgy that is celebrated in heaven in the presence of the angels.

Letter of the Holy See addressed to the President of the *Pro Liturgia* Association (Rosheim).

[2] In the same diocese, in the same parish, there are as many ways of celebrating Mass as there are priests: each of them interprets the Roman Missal in his own fashion . . . The television viewer who follows along with the Mass every Sunday as it is broadcast on the program called "The Lord's Day" is apt to have a rough idea of the number of variations on the Mass that can be found in the churches; the same television viewer, if he has a missal in hand, will also realize that rarely, if ever, is the liturgy of the Church truly respected.

The Fact of Believing or Teaching that the Old Liturgy Would Provide the Faithful with Shelter from Theological Errors and that It Would Be a Defense against Doctrinal Deviations

Affirmations of this kind betray a total ignorance of the history of the liturgy, which amply demonstrates that the so-called rite "of Saint Pius V" prevented neither Gallicanism nor Josephism, nor the erring ways of a Father Meslier and many others, nor the broken, limping liturgy encountered by Dom Guéranger even in the nineteenth century, nor the abandonment of Gregorian chant and its replacement by the plain chant of Versailles, by the German "*Singmesse*", or by the hymns of Saint Sulpice. Nor did it prevent the schism of the Old Catholics, and so on. Even to this day, the old rites are jealously preserved by the Gallican Church (St. Rita's church, Paris), which rejects the dogma of papal infallibility.

No, the old liturgy cannot guarantee sound doctrine on the part of its participants any more than can the new liturgy for that matter.[3] It was this very thing to which

---

[3] "It must be recognized that the application of the liturgical reform has met with difficulties. . . . Different and even contradictory reactions to the reform have resulted from this. Some have received the new books with a certain indifference or without trying to understand or help others to understand the reasons for the changes; others, unfortunately, have turned back in a one-sided and exclusive way to the previous liturgical forms, which some of them consider to be the sole guarantee of certainty in faith" (John Paul II, the letter *Vicesimus quintus annus* [December 4, 1988], no. 11, in *The Pope Speaks* 34 [September-October 1989]: 227).

Father André-Vincent drew attention in an issue of the journal *Una Voce*:

> The fundamental condition of the Catholic liturgy consists of the sacramental words and faith in these divinely inspired words. To be sure, Loisy and many others celebrated the "traditional Mass", while giving the same meaning to the text as they would today if they used the "Mass of Paul VI". They read the "narrative" of the Last Supper in the traditional rite as they would have read it in the new rite. The words of Consecration are a part of the narrative. For them these words were no more than a mere narrative. They may have read them with piety, even a deep respect. But all the same, these words were merely something they read. . . . The Words of the sacrament remained a mere narrative and not an act of Christ. . . . The drama of our current situation is to be found reflected in their case. The evil is in their want of faith, not in the texts. A papal decree ordering a return to the old [preconciliar] Canon (supposing that it was issued and obeyed) would be stripped of its meaning and intent if it fell on the stony ground of modernism. The evil here is of a theological order. It lies in the realm of theology.[4]

Moreover, there is an undeniable fact that should make us reflect: it has often been priests formed under the old liturgy in the seminaries predating Vatican II who have done the most, in the wake of the Council, to alter and falsify the restored liturgy, making a sudden, jarring about-face from rigidity to a total casualness and lack of restraint.

---

[4] *Una Voce* 109 (March-April 1993), quoted by Franck Lafarge, *Du refus au schisme: Le traditionalisme catholique* (From disobedience to schism: Catholic traditionalism)] (Paris: Éd. du Seuil, 1988).

Also, in our own day, who is most often to be found at the head of the diocesan "liturgical commissions" that have given rise to the anarchy we have experienced? It is precisely the priests who were scrupulously formed under the old liturgy and who, quite often, before the Council, would never have allowed anyone the liberty of touching the rites. In yesterday's world no less than today's, these clerics have made the mistake of seeing "religious practice as something of a private affair"[5] and believing that they have ownership of the rites of the Church. This only goes to show that, although the Council wanted to change certain attitudes, it did not always succeed in weakening the hold of clericalism, that is to say, the triumph of power on the part of human institutions instead of service on behalf of the divine Institution.

The Need for Emotional Security

Because it was rigorously codified, the old liturgy offered a kind of security. When a person went to church to assist at Mass, he knew that there he was going to find a "ceremony-type" identified with the eucharistic liturgy. And inasmuch as this was a time when the prayers said by the celebrant were not heard, attention was fixed on the unchanging, exterior forms of the act of worship: the white gloves of the bishop, the pastor's lacework alb, the ringing of the bells at the elevation, the singing of a particular hymn at Midnight Mass, the slap given by

---

[5] John Paul II, *Vicesimus quintus annus*, no. 11; see also no. 12, in *Pope Speaks*, 227.

the bishop at the ceremony of confirmation, the clink-
ing of the chains on the thurible, and so on. When the
neo-liturgists did away with all of this, they deprived
many of the faithful of the secure points of reference that
they had invested with an eternal significance solely because these were the points of reference they had always
known.

Nevertheless, it must be confessed that these neo-
liturgists were often crass demolitionists who were hardly
shining stars when it came to a proper sense of pedagogy.
They forgot that man is not pure spirit and that he needs
sensory points of reference, especially in the realm of worship, where it is a question of evoking spiritual realities
that are inexpressible. It was a good thing to abolish certain elements of the eucharistic rite, the significance of
which risked being distorted by the romanticism or sentimentality that the liturgy had inherited from the nineteenth century—sometimes even by a residual Jansenism
—provided they knew how to replace them with something better. This was what the Council wanted. However, by going beyond the wise directives of Vatican II
in the process of jettisoning excess baggage, certain neo-
liturgists embarked on a cruel destruction of the rituals.
By mutilating the liturgy, this destruction ended in a void
or a desert, or in infantilism. At that point, the faithful,
for want of sacred signs, spontaneously went searching
in other churches for what they had been denied in their
respective parishes. And this is quite understandable on
their part.

Nationalist Sentiments

Nobody can deny that in certain places the Mass "of Saint Pius V" has a nationalist coloring that does not correspond to what the faithful have the right to expect from a Catholic celebration. In many gatherings and meetings, the rituals of the old Roman liturgy become an occasion to give voice, through the Church, to an ideology that is not in keeping with authentic, Christian doctrine. And, not to put too fine a point on it, it is obvious that "Tridentine" liturgies are also (not solely, but also) used by people who tend to the extreme right politically, just as other celebrations in so-called "workers' parishes" are strongly colored by the ideological preoccupations of revolutionary organizations.[6]

The Attempt to Alleviate the Discontent of the Faithful by "Traditionalist" Movements: A Tactical Error?

Nobody can deny that the liturgy today is in a state of grave crisis, especially in the countries of "old Christianity", like France. Now the seriousness of this situation does not lie so much in the crisis itself as in the silence of the bishops in the face of this crisis: a silence that has lasted forty years! As a result, because the pastors of dioceses have undertaken to do almost nothing to counteract a crisis that they are not unaware of, the faithful have turned to movements that advocate a return to the old liturgy, claiming that they have a right to this option. This

---

[6] Dom Jean-Marie Pommarès, *Notitiae*, no. 357 (April 1996).

temptation to take refuge in "traditionalist" movements is not without danger. Why so?

a. Because none of these movements guarantees the total absence of sometimes ambiguous collusions between the spiritual and the temporal. In such cases the preconciliar liturgy (the so-called Mass "of Saint Pius V") can become, as was mentioned earlier, the focus of an orientation that is more political than simply liturgical.

b. Because, in referring to the Mass, these movements use terms or expressions that do not correspond to the truth of the "liturgical fact", as we saw at the beginning of this study. Strange, heterogeneous mixtures of fact and vague, historical approximations can only sow confusion in the minds of a good number of the faithful as well as division in the bosom of the Church.

c. Because it is false to maintain that the preservation of the old liturgy is a right. There are no allowances made for the preservation of the old liturgy either in the Council's Constitution (cf. nos. 3 and 4) or in the Indult *Ecclesia Dei adflicta* given by Pope John Paul II on July 2, 1988, following the schism of Archbishop Lefebvre, even though "traditionalist" movements make constant reference to this Indult.

This being the case, if there is an earnest desire to rescue the liturgy from the crisis in which it is mired, things should be seen in a different light and the current situation should be subjected to a better analysis.

It is well known that the main objective set for themselves by those in charge of "traditionalist" associations is to achieve the establishment in each diocese of at least one regular celebration of the Mass according to the Missal of 1962, the so-called Mass "of Saint Pius V".

On the one hand, this request is based on the indult promulgated in 1988 following the schism of Archbishop Lefebvre. By means of this indult, Pope John Paul II in fact opened up the possibility of using the old liturgical texts. In issuing it, he stressed that it should be generously applied by the bishops under certain well-specified conditions. On the other hand, this request is also based on the report, unfortunately all too real and readily verifiable, that many people who no longer find in most churches what they have the full right to expect from the point of view of liturgy are turning more and more to the old rite such as it existed right to the time of the Second Vatican Council.

Therefore, the question must be asked: What will be the eventual outcome of this project, which appears so straightforward?

Two scenarios present themselves:

In the first, the places that have been thus obtained for the celebration of the old liturgy become something like "ghetto-chapels". To be sure, all those who explicitly seek out the old rite will be found there. But there will also be many believers justly dissatisfied with the way the Council has been applied in their parishes. The latter will have been sent there to be gotten rid of, as it were. How exquisitely simple it is, in fact, for the bishop of a diocese

who wants to pass for "a man of openness and dialogue",
to offer them a place of worship! The many empty and
unused churches offer a perfect solution for the attempt
to satisfy once and for all those who have been disap-
pointed by the Council. But in reality are we not dealing
here with an easy way out that has been chosen in order to
establish a quarantine against the current liturgy and thus
avoid its being celebrated in the parishes? Is it not a means
that permits diocesan officials to have a clear conscience
about "traditionalists" even as they avoid having to correct the current situation? Even as they avoid questioning themselves and especially questioning the countless
diocesan agencies charged with "pastoral liturgy", agencies that would lose their reason for existing overnight,
if it were decided quite simply and plainly to apply the
directives of the Council?

And then one day, demanding that the chapel be closed
for some makeshift pastoral reason (since the chapel is
only open by force of an indult and is thus at the mercy
of a temporary "generosity"), the diocesan authorities
know that they can, in a single stroke, get rid of all the an-
noying "embarrassments", including not only those who
are attached to the old liturgy but also those who are
simply attached to the liturgy of Vatican II and the use
of Latin and Gregorian chant, according to the teaching
of the Council.

Therefore, we can hardly do other than reject a situation of this kind, which leads inevitably to the death of
the liturgy, precisely insofar as we believe in the grandeur
and the beauty of the liturgy as restored by the Coun-

cil and insofar as we know that we must work, in the Church, for a true birth at last of this Roman liturgy, so that it may be developed and become a living presence in all our parishes, as expressly requested by Pope John Paul II.[7]

In a second scenario, these places in which the old liturgy is celebrated are going to attract congregations deprived of an authentic liturgy. Such places will multiply and flourish, for a time, at any rate, establishing the preconciliar liturgy in a permanent way, with the same legitimacy and the same prospects as the renewed liturgy. Perhaps in our dioceses here in France we will even see the old ordo supplanting the new, thus creating a kind of ruinous neo-Gallicanism!

This situation is no longer one that is not really imaginable, even though it contradicts, as we have seen, the first function of the promulgation of the indult *Ecclesia Dei adflicta*, which permits the use of the Missal of 1962 only in certain well-defined cases. It should be recalled that the indult is aimed at those who feel so greatly disoriented by the speed with which changes were introduced at the time of the Council or by the apparent disrespect inherent in these changes that their faith suffers harm. The first function of the indult is to allow people who feel this way to reimmerse themselves in the past for a time, using this as an opportunity to find a pathway to the future in serenity and calm at their own rate of speed. But never has the Church questioned the necessity for

---

[7] *Vicesimus quintus annus*, nos. 13–14.

the liturgical modifications that have taken place or the legitimacy of the so-called missal ''of Paul VI''. Rather everyone is called to forge ahead and not to go backward or embrace a fixed state of changelessness in order to take refuge in an idealized past.

CHAPTER SIX

Ongoing Difficulties

The present study has made it possible to show the sheer magnitude of the current liturgical crisis. But in view of the extent of the crisis, other vital considerations enter into play. Many of the faithful have indeed given thought to them. They can be condensed into two headings: straight facts and consequences.

The Straight Facts

The Virtual Nonexistence of the Eucharistic Liturgy Celebrated according to the Official Rituals

The faithful who are informed report that, in current circumstances, it has become impossible, so to speak, on the parish level, to participate in a Sunday Eucharist celebrated as required by the official liturgical books published in the wake of the Second Vatican Council (books such as the Roman Missal, the Ceremonial of Bishops, and so on).

The Silence or Tactlessness of Bishops When Dealing with Well-Defined Liturgical Questions that Come under Their Sole Authority

The faithful who are attached to the application of conciliar directives where the liturgy is concerned have noted with bitter sadness that:

— when their legitimate requests dealing with respect for the rituals established by the Church are addressed to the pastors of dioceses, they meet with blunt refusals or stalling tactics;

— pastors have never put a stop to the deviations that have been disseminated by numerous publications (*Fiches liturgiques du diocèse de Saint-Brieuc* [Liturgical notes from the diocese of Saint-Brieuc], the journal *Signe d'aujourd'hui* [Sign of the times], and so on). Even though they enjoy no official recognition, these publications have been introduced into the parishes on a very broad scale as substitutes for the Roman Missal and are used both by celebrants and liturgical teams to make more or less serious changes to the liturgy of the Church. In this way, they concoct dubious celebrations, which are imposed on the faithful;

— pastors have never been prepared to concede that there is an obligation, on the part of every celebrant, to conform faithfully and honestly to the liturgical rules given in the Roman Missal.

The Ongoing, Widespread Nature of the Abuses

The faithful note that:

— in many dioceses in France, the bishops themselves have given a bad example either by improvising the liturgy in whole or in part or by using loose-leaf binders and laminated or photocopied sheets by way of a missal;

— in diocesan seminaries bishops tolerate liturgical abuses but punish candidates for the priesthood who want to respect the current Roman Missal;

— whole sections of the eucharistic liturgy have fallen into neglect and disuse by virtue of having been systematically omitted in celebrations: the penitential rite, the *Gloria*, the Creed, the *Agnus Dei*, the washing of the hands, the embolism that follows the Our Father, liturgical vestments, the use of incense, and so on;

— the few priests who conform to the official, liturgical books to celebrate the Eucharist have sometimes been ousted and relieved of all public ministry on the pretext that their fidelity to the liturgical norms betrays a "Roman mind-set" on their part and is not in agreement with the orientations of the "diocesan pastoral program".

The Problem of the So-Called "Tridentine" Liturgy
or Liturgy "of Saint Pius V"

The faithful report that those who, in all fairness and justice, desire to participate in a dignified and prayerful liturgy, one that is respectful of the ritual and quite legal and possibly celebrated in its Latin and Gregorian form, are sent systematically by their pastors to the "traditionalist" chapels where the so-called Mass "of Saint Pius V" is celebrated.

Attached to these chapels all too often are groups that dispute the validity of the liturgy that was restored following the Second Vatican Council.

This habit of sending to "ghetto-chapels" those of the faithful whose only wish is to participate in the liturgy of the Church as it should be celebrated in our day and age has given birth to a strange coalition consisting of those who desire a sincere application of Vatican II and those who dispute the orientations of the Council. From this we get the ongoing confusions and dissensions that do serious harm to the unity of the Church.

The Consequences

For all the reasons enumerated above, it can be stated that those of the faithful who are truly and sincerely attached to an authentic eucharistic liturgy these days have been thrust, despite themselves, into a veritable liturgical no-man's land, which allows a person only three possibilities:

— to participate in celebrations that have more or less gone astray, the rites of which are often hijacked in favor of an immediate, simple satisfaction of feelings;

— or else to take refuge in "ghetto chapels" where the celebrations are carried out by adhering closely to the rites and usages that predate Vatican II. This seems to situate the whole problem in an old Gallican tradition that tends more and more to lessen the visible manifestations of the universality of the Church;

— or else to cease all practice of religion while waiting in expectation of being able one day to find churches where the celebrant holds fast to the current Roman Missal.

In all these cases, the outcome is that the faithful feel deeply frustrated and hurt, to the point where they are no longer able to derive the slightest spiritual benefit from the celebration. For, by their fidelity to the reiterated teachings of the Holy Father, many of the faithful are unwilling and unable by their presence and their participation to endorse

— either the "unpredictable" liturgies that are currently celebrated in a majority of parish churches

— or the "Tridentine" liturgies (also known as Masses "of Saint Pius V"), which, even though legitimate in certain cases, are currently used by diocesan pastors to erect a veritable "quarantine" against the Roman liturgy that was restored following Vatican II.[1]

---

[1] These facts and their consequences were reported during the general assembly of the *Pro Liturgia* Association that was held in Paris in 1996.

CHAPTER SEVEN

Conclusion

At the same time as it reveals and celebrates the objective faith of the whole Church, liturgical ritual accomplishes a triple function:

— it "structures" man by giving him his exact place, his individual and social status, in such a way that he can freely achieve self-determination in the face of spiritual realities;

— it "channels" the main threads of thought and feeling that allow the believer to confront divine realities;

— it "protects" the believer from possible pathological components in the group that has gathered to celebrate the faith of the Church.

Knowing this, we can better understand that the Second Vatican Council asked a twofold question:

— First of all, would the old rites of the Mass (the so-called rite "of Saint Pius V", for instance) have still been capable of "structuring", "channeling", and "protecting" the believer? The answer here is in the negative: the old liturgy, as we have seen, was made up of a certain number of disparate elements that had not seemed "shocking" at the time they were first intro-duced. But these elements, when combined with the insipid tastes that were fostered by the Sulpician style in the nineteenth century and by neo-romanticism, would no longer have been able to respond to the current requirements of the Christian faith without running the risk of stifling the human person. The Church, therefore, could not have dispensed with a liturgical renewal.

— Second, we turn to the Masses that are said nowa-days ostensibly with the authority of the Council but that are not—it must be stressed—in conformity with the liturgy as restored by Vatican II, no matter what our pastors say. Are these Masses capable of "struc-turing", "channeling", and "protecting" the believer? Here, once more, the answer is in the negative. There have been all too many interruptions, too many words, too many hymns, too many idiosyncratic adjustments that have been added to our present-day liturgies. All these things are signs of a subjectivism that has made dangerous incursions into our celebrations, emptying them of their content, hindering any attempt to struc-ture the human person. In the form in which they are presently celebrated, certain liturgies can even become dangerous for the spiritual and psychological equilib-rium of believers. Without a faith-filled vision, wrote Cardinal Danneels, the liturgy makes no sense: it re-sembles nothing so much as a strange piece of "second-rate theatre'' that is so shabby and pathetic that there is certainly no justification for attending it every Sunday (*sic*). Perhaps, as things stand, we should go one step farther in our analysis of current liturgies and ask whether certain celebrations, quite apart from being instances of shabby, ''second-rate theatre'', run the risk as well of becoming ''harmful sideshows''? Are not certain liturgies transformed into harmful sideshows when the participants in the celebration decide to play a role that is different from the one that is properly theirs? What happens when the priest, instead of celebrating the Eucharist, is constantly indulging in explanations and giving commentaries? When, instead of *singing the Mass*, the choir *sings at the Mass* and gives a concert? When, instead of helping the liturgy to unfold unobtrusively, the director holds center stage? When, instead of providing an aid to prayer, the organist gives a recital? When these things happen, the liturgy is subjected to serious distortions: instead of forming a homogeneous whole that is balanced and balancing, it becomes a succession of events in which each of the people involved tries to add a personal touch. The believer can no longer apprehend the liturgy in its totality and its unity, for the rite takes on the appearance of being ruptured, as it were, composed of disjointed elements that follow one another without rhyme or reason in a totally arbitrary fashion. The result of this is a depressing sense of heaviness that can become a source of tension, generating a real feeling of uneasiness and disquiet.

Are not certain current-day Masses "harmful side-shows", even when they are replete with beautiful hymns, beautiful vestments, incense, and an attitude of relative respect for the rituals? The external beauty of the celebration should never serve to foster a sense of illusion, and it should always be asked what are the real reasons prompting a celebrant to maintain a certain decorum. Is this decorum (often confused with the integrity of the liturgical action) dictated by a desire to enhance the liturgy in order to give glory to God and sanctify the faithful, or is it only maintained to satisfy personal tastes? Is it prompted by the sincere desire to aid the public prayer of the Church in an objective way, or is it only maintained for the purpose of satisfying the passionate concerns of some particular participant in the celebration? Does it proceed from a concern for the truth that lies in the form of the liturgy, or does it betray a desire to make a spectacular impression? There are presently celebrations that could be described as confused and disordered because the rituals, even when they are respected, have been corrupted, as it were: they are no longer preserved for their own intrinsic value but merely because they serve to put the spotlight on the participants in the liturgy. Rather than turning our focus to the Essence of what is happening at the altar, these celebrations focus our attention on those who bustle busily around the altar, those who use the splendors of the ritual to make their bid for the limelight. Now when, in a eucharistic celebration, people lose sight of the Essence in favor of personal interests, the liturgy in its entirety quickly risks

becoming not only an instance of "second-rate theatre",
but even a "harmful sideshow": a sideshow that is apt to
be dazzling for a stretch of time but shows itself incapable,
over the longer term, of bringing comfort, satisfaction,
and serenity. We should, therefore, be constantly making
sure that it is genuine faith that is our reason for attending to the liturgy in a spirit of zeal and submission and
not our desire to please a given congregation or satisfy
personal feelings. For each one of us ought to be able to
acknowledge that it is the living Christ who is the prime
mover and end of the liturgical act, and not the individualism of the one who is appointed to perform a ministry
(cf. Saint Paul to the Galatians, 2:19–21).

The "non-liturgy" in its current state, the constant,
drastic fluctuation between anachronistic rites and shapeless, uncertain liturgies, has had its effect on the faithful. Even though the faithful do not always know how
to express their expectations, even though all too often
they believe that a eucharistic celebration whose ceremonial aspects are pleasing to them conforms to the ritual
standards, many of them sense deep within themselves a
profound dissatisfaction engendered by their attendance
at present-day Masses. Thus, little by little, they are becoming aware that the future well-being of the Church
will inevitably be brought about through a sincere respect
for the authentic liturgy, which is the "source and sum-
mit of the life of the Church",[1] even though they have no

---

[1] Vatican II, the Constitution on the Sacred Liturgy, *Sacrosanctum
concilium* (December 4, 1963), no. 10.

precise idea of the way in which this "authentic liturgy" should be made manifest. Nowadays there is a "thirst for authenticity".

That is why the faithful should take note of the persistent and generalized nature of the deviations, so often arbitrary, in the way that the Eucharist is celebrated. They need to note, too, the alarming drop in attendance at Sunday Mass in the parishes and to see that a younger generation, which is sincere in its search for the sacred and enjoys a heightened appreciation of the notion of dignity, is turning more and more to preconciliar forms of the liturgy (the so-called rite "of Saint Pius V"), precisely because it has not been given the appropriate means to participate in the present-day liturgy. With these things in mind, the faithful who have never questioned the decisions taken by the Second Vatican Council need to address themselves anew to their bishops. With all the filial respect that is due their bishops, but insistently, they should ask them to be willing at long last to institute measures that will guarantee to one and all the celebration of the eucharistic liturgy such as it appears in the current Roman Missal. This request would apply as much to the liturgy's legitimate vernacular forms as to its Latin, Gregorian form, without additions or omissions or modifications or even simplifications imposed for reasons that are ostensibly "pastoral".

Except that there is a problem. For the bishops to be able "to institute measures" that would promote respect for the liturgy, for them to be able—to use the words of John Paul II—"to root out the abuses" that have been introduced and generalized in celebrations, they will need a great deal of lucidity and courage. They will need lucidity, on the one hand, to see the real sources of the problem, namely, the diocesan bureaucracies, the commissions, the teams of liturgical facilitators—all those structures that Cardinal Ratzinger described as "useless". And they will need courage, on the other hand, to denounce those responsible, within what amounts to an interdiocesan *"nomenklatura"*, for encouraging falsifications of the liturgy by using journals sustained by solidly established networks of financial support.

Unhappily, it must be acknowledged that those of the faithful who believe they can find real courage in their bishops are becoming fewer and fewer in number. Why this lack of confidence? There are two essential reasons. The first is that many bishops give the impression that they have replaced their "pastoral authority" with "arbitrary pressure". The bishops exercise this "pressure" by relying—probably as much for reasons of expediency as of weakness—on power that is strictly ideological, power that is jealously maintained and exercised by diocesan bureaucrats. This pressure, moreover, is used against clerics and laypeople who dare to denounce the closed shop of the diocesan structures. For the bishop is well aware that if he gets rid of these structures in order to give credence to the arguments of the faithful who denounce the dysfunctional nature of the current pastoral apparatus, he will be making himself new enemies in the heart of his own *presbyterium*.[2] The second reason is that for the past

---

[2] See Patrick Chalmel, *Ecône ou Rome: Le Choix de Pierre* (Paris: Fayard, 1990), 37ff. The author speaks of bishops being "terrorized" by

forty years certain bishops have given the impression that they are only prepared to make declarations that are "pastorally correct" and to issue soothing discourses on social questions for which, to put it bluntly, they have neither the competence nor the authority. But, by way of contrast, they are no longer heard using strong words to tackle real spiritual problems with a deep sense of conviction, when it is precisely these problems that fall within their competence and about which people expect them to make pronouncements.

A few examples will suffice to illustrate these observations. No sooner had the faithful taken it upon themselves to publish some serious catechetical manuals than did the bishops, held fast in the web of their all-powerful authorities, order the destruction of these books, on the pretext that they had not been approved by the official commissions. At the same time, our shepherds were congratulating one another for bringing out *Pierres vivantes* (Living stones), a manual that, besides being a financial "scam", turned out to be a fiasco despite the collaboration of theologians and educators and despite the expensive publicity campaign that had been lavished on it. No sooner did the faithful wish to participate in a Mass celebrated with an attitude of respect toward the missal restored by the Council than this Mass was forbidden on the pretext that the liturgy was not properly integrated with the "diocesan pastoral plan" or that it "risked car-

---

commissions or diocesan bureaucracies, admitting that they "can do nothing about it".

rying too great a baggage of exemplification'' (*sic*).[3] No sooner did the faithful express their desire to travel in order to greet the Pope on his visit to France than they were made to understand that it was pointless for them to come in too great a number. No sooner did the laity organize a tour of France for their statues of our Lady than did the bishops speak out to denounce such practices, which stemmed from another age and had no official mandate.[4] No sooner did the faithful denounce a priest or a theologian whose sermons and conferences were riddled with heresies than the bishop raised his voice: not to put the priest or theologian in question in his place, but to silence the person who dared, in the name of his Catholic faith, to give vent to a criticism that was directed at an ''untouchable''. To strike hammer blows against faith and doctrine is actually less serious than wounding the dignity of one of the bishop's favorites . . .[5] No sooner did the faithful denounce the Comité Catholique contre la Faim et pour le Développement[6] for teaming up with Marxist movements than did our bishops react in full cry, claiming this to be a calumny. We would have

---

[3] On the question of the liturgy and the power of bureaucracies, it would be profitable to reread J. C. Didelot's book *Clérocratie dans l'Église de France* (Paris: Fayard, 1991), 153ff.

[4] In Poland, it was the episcopate as a whole that organized a welcome for the pilgrim Virgins; this occasioned great ceremonies. Yes, but Poland is not France, as we all know!

[5] Let us cite the example of the archbishop who, to "protect" a priest charged with numerous diocesan responsibilities, said that he was in agreement with the thesis upheld by this same priest, in which it is clearly written that the Mass is not a sacrifice.

[6] Catholic Committee against Hunger and for Development.

to await the discreet intervention of Archbishop Decourtray of Lyons, to hear it said officially that there were instances of collusion between the Church in France and the communist left.

In April 1991 there took place in Rome a symposium on the teaching of religion in public schools. All the episcopal conferences in the Catholic Church met together— twenty-one delegations all together. The delegation representing the French conference of bishops was the only one not to vote for the final resolution adopted by this symposium, which recommended the institution of religious instruction along confessional lines, according to the German and Italian model, in the public educational system of all the European states.[7]

In November 1996 a new fact came to attest that in the "Church as it exists in France" the problems are approached almost systematically from the wrong end. Gathered together at Lourdes from November 4 to November 9, the bishops once again made the observation that the Church has a shortage of priests. This is hardly earth-shattering news. One might have hoped that the bishops would confidently use this assessment as a point of departure to call into question the way in which seminaries are currently run and to take as their model the institutions that are attracting young people today. This is certainly not what happened. Rather, the argument ran, we have a shortage of priests . . . therefore, we had better

[7] Guy Coq, *Laïcité et République*, cited by Pierre-Philippe Bayant, who is in charge of formation at the chaplaincy of the public board of education in Alsace, in *Saisons d'Alsace*, 1996, 95ff.

think about ordaining more permanent deacons and appointing certain laypeople to administer the sacraments. Here we have a new way for those who are desperately keen to rise in the social ranks to enter the institution in order to appear elite members of a privileged circle.[8] In many respects some of those in charge of the Church in France have managed to give the impression that they are playing a bizarre joke on us—either that, or they do not really understand the seriousness of the situation or the expectations of the real "people in the pew", who are leaving the churches on tiptoe. But is there not at the root of this present pastoral situation an ideology that favors the impulse to construct a new Church: a Church with neither liturgy nor priesthood, a Church that is a kind of nebulous, spiritual no-man's land in which every person can build himself a nice, little faith world of his own, one that corresponds to his tastes and feelings? This is the question we must ask ourselves, whenever we are told, in the official diocesan publications, that we must "dare to construct a new model of the Church".

There are many who, when they see all this happening and appreciate the magnitude of the disaster that has overtaken us in the last forty years or so, are prompted at length to ask themselves an agonizing question, a question that must, when all is said and done, be voiced: To what extent is it still possible to trust our bishops to give us from this moment on in all our churches the liturgy as

---

[8] When Bishop Gaillot was being removed from office in the diocese of Evreux, it was clear to see the role that was played in this affair by the many permanent deacons and laymen in positions of responsibility who opposed the decisions of the Vatican.

it appears in the Roman Missal that was restored in the wake of Vatican II? In France, it seems that the hierarchy of bishops is exclusively preoccupied with protecting a system over which in actual fact it no longer has any control. Indeed, it is at the heart of this system that we find the real *apparatchiks* of the liturgical arm of pastoral theology. By confiscating the liturgy of the Church, they have deprived the faithful of their first source of sanctification. This being the case, is it not time to affirm, with Cardinal Ratzinger, "that a real reform of the Church presupposes an unequivocal turning away from the erroneous paths whose catastrophic consequences are already incontestable"?[9]

> To be sure, the Church will always need new human structures in order to give herself a framework and the capability, as well, to speak and work in every era of history. These ecclesiastical institutions—and the juridical aspects that come with them—are far from being representative of something evil. Rather, they are, in a certain way, simply necessary and indispensable. But, as they grow older, they run the risk of appearing to be of prime importance and of deflecting attention away from what is essential. This is the reason why they should be continuously dismantled as just so much scaffolding that has become superfluous. . . . It is not a more human Church that we need, but rather a more divine Church, for this is how she will also be truly human.[10]

---

[9] Joseph Cardinal Ratzinger with Vittorio Messori, *The Ratzinger Report: An Exclusive Interview on the State of the Church*, trans. Salvator Attanasio and Graham Harrison (San Francisco: Ignatius Press, 1985), 30.

[10] *Communio* 16, 1 (January-February 1991).

What we expect from the shepherds of our dioceses is the courage that comes from surrender and abandonment to the Lord. What the Church needs in order to respond to the needs of man in his quest for the Absolute are not management skills[11] but sanctity and strongly stated beliefs.[12] And as for the specific problem of the liturgy, we expect that our bishops will give us, at long last, after years of aberrations,[13] the "normative Mass" as it is pre-

---

[11] "Nowadays, when, in order to explain the difficulties encountered by the liturgical reform, prelates or experts advert to the fact that the reform has not been adequately explained, it is because they have forgotten the huge avalanche of writings, homilies, and commentaries of all kinds that overwhelmed the faithful after the Council for almost ten years. It is true, however, that these various writings were not in fact sufficient, for the philosophy that informed the changes that were being implemented was part and parcel of a problematic syndrome that plagued the ranks of the clergy or rather, one might say, clericalized intellectuals" Claude Barthe, *Trouvera-t-il encore la foi sur la terre? Une Crise de l'Église: Histoire et questions* (Paris: F. X. de Guibert, 1996), 168.

[12] According to Cardinal Ratzinger, *Ratzinger Report*, 67.

[13] In the issue of *Documentation Catholique* for February 4, 1996, Bishop Moutel, in a "Letter to the Bishops of France", makes the observation that the musical compositions currently in use for eucharistic celebrations are "poor, unclear, and not sufficient to nurture a proper expression of faith". In the issue of *Esprit et Vie* (no. 10) for March 7, 1996, Archbishop Jullien writes that, "in our communities the splitting off into factions serves to highlight a liturgical deficit, an impoverishment as regards signs, a negligent disregard for the symbolic, an ignorance of the realm of aesthetics, and even, here and there, a denial of the legitimate forms taken by the prayer of the Church, which we have no right to change. This phenomenon forces us to return the elements of authentic, religious expression to their just place in the liturgy." And farther on in his piece the Archbishop of Rennes adds: "Experience shows that where service of the community is not institutionalized, it risks being harnessed by leaders who confuse power with service. New communities are sometimes worried about being confused with

scribed in detail in the actual missal. Only this Mass—
which is still officially rejected on French territory except
by certain monasteries[14] and some few parishes that can
be considered privileged in the circumstances that pre-
vail these days—can reconcile Christians who have been
divided or have become indifferent about the sacrament
that is the flowing source of the Church's true greatness,
not to mention her holiness and unity. This is the truth, it
seems, that a whole new generation of priests have come
to understand perfectly well, for they have shown by and
large that they are more concerned about liturgical norms.
The parishes that fall under the responsibility of this new
breed of priests have come to experience an undeniable
renewal of vitality.

Certainly this does not mean that young people are
better than their elders. Rather, this merely goes to show
that the new generation of priests, which has not lived
through the Council, is not encumbered by the rearguard
actions that were fought in the wake of Vatican II. The
situation, moreover, is aptly described by John Paul II:

> The liturgy of the Church goes beyond the liturgical re-
> form. We are not in the same situation as we were in
> 1963: A generation of priests and of faithful which has
> not known the liturgical books prior to the reform now

---

sects. Is this not an invitation to new communities to avoid anything
that could foster confusion in the minds of the faithful? For example,
in the way they dress or their liturgical expression, or if they have an
undue preoccupation with miraculous phenomena.''

[14] Solesmes, Saint-Wandrille, Kergonan, Saint Eustase, etc.

acts with responsibility in the Church and society. One cannot therefore continue to speak of change as it was spoken of at the time of the constitution's publication; rather one has to speak of an ever deeper grasp of the liturgy of the Church, celebrated according to the current books and lived above all as a reality in the spiritual order.[15]

Nevertheless, the new situation as it unfolds will not be without certain problems. These include the issues of collaboration with the pastors of other parishes and collaboration with liturgical teams that were put in place before the arrival of the new priests, teams that have been won over by ideas promoted in journals specializing, with a "progressive slant", in the "pastoral theology of the liturgy", and so on. But it cannot be denied that the study sessions that are taking place these days and that have as their theme respect for the current liturgy or the study of Gregorian chant, as restored by the recent research efforts undertaken by the Benedictines at Solesmes, attract more young priests and seminarians than they do clerics of the older generation.[16] This is why, perhaps, we have a real reason to hope for a new springtime of the liturgy, without, however, denying that things will not be restored to their proper place without difficulties. In the near future, to be sure, bishops will need a vivid pastoral sense in order to support some members of their flock without

---

[15] *Vicesimus quintus annus* (December 4, 1988), no. 14, in *The Pope Speaks* 34 (September-October 1989): 228.

[16] This is the case, for example, at liturgical formation sessions organized at the Kergonan Abbey by the *Pro Liturgia* Association.

offending others and to channel the new forces that have come into play without wounding certain older priests who have already given a lot in the service of a Church that was caught up in the raging storm that came in the wake of the Council.

Appendix

Some Testimonies:

FROM A YOUNG PRIEST

The liturgy is not a matter of sensibilities but of faith. As proof of this I draw your attention to the page that I have enclosed with this letter. It has to do with a diocesan proposal for a celebration (and as such sanctioned by the authority of the bishop!). According to it, parish priests are asked to celebrate "life's happenings" without any mention being made of the sacrifice of the Lord. How should a person react to this? I am a young priest, just an assistant to the pastor. I've been lucky so far to have been in peaceful parishes, without being saddled with the problem of clericalized laypeople. But there are many priests of my generation who have precious little room to maneuver if they want to celebrate the true liturgy, as required by Vatican II. For this reason there are many of them whose only desire is to return to the so-called Mass "of Saint Pius V". Whose fault is this? For many, the French bishops and even more so the numerous commissions and other committees that the bishops have set up and that they can no longer control are caught up in a crisis that has deprived the faithful of the true liturgical prayer of the Church.

I conclude this letter by asking you to say a fervent prayer for young diocesan priests, since many of them have to suffer through Calvary-like experiences that are difficult to imagine.

FROM A YOUNG PRIEST

I am writing to inform you about two pastoral difficulties that I have encountered in my ministry and that I also see as being very widespread around me.

The first concerns the altars in the churches. After my ordination, I was put in charge of several country parishes. Now in all these parish churches there are *ancient*, marble *altars*, dating from the last century or the eighteenth century, and there are *new altars* made from wooden boards that have been crudely slapped together (in one case, the paint on the boards is chipped, the boards themselves having been salvaged from the demolition of a shed; in another case, the altar is a piece of furniture from the sacristy, half worm-eaten and covered by a bedsheet fastened with staples. . . .)

What to do? For the clergy and faithful such arrangements have become commonplace. They don't even see that there's a problem. It would come as a surprise to more than one of them if you brought it to their attention that all these sorts of things are not good, that they do not do justice to the celebration of the Eucharist.

I find it especially noteworthy that the faithful obviously regard only the *old altar* as important. It is the old altar that they take care of and treat with respect. The only problem is that many do not want Mass to be celebrated on it, simply because they have been told time and again that this would be a "step backward" and a sign of "integralism" (in this respect I am duty-bound to stress that the problem of the proper liturgical formation of the laity is enormous, for so many of those involved in their formation merely pass on their subjective prejudices).

Of course, none of the parishioners would accept the disappearance of the *old altars*, even though these altars have only a relative value. Is this attitude not significant in some way or other?

Are we going to be forced to keep two altars in rural churches, which are often smaller in size? If so, we are putting the brakes on all liturgical development and trapping ourselves in a provisional situation. This question is all the more important insofar as, generally speaking, there is a reluctance to install a second fixed altar in these churches on the grounds that there should be nothing to detract from the aesthetics of the place and that nothing should be done that would render the staging of concerts impossible (hence we get a dangerous shift in meaning and outlook, requiring the sacred place of the liturgy to be adaptable to concerts). Many of the churches in our area have, at best, an office desk, a sacristy table, or a kitchen table . . . as an altar. In conditions like these, how do the minds of the faithful hold fast to the true meaning of the eucharistic celebration or, more broadly, the liturgy (*lex orandi, lex credendi*)? As a priest, I think this problem is important enough to be the subject of a full-length study. If in the near future there is no renewal of the sense of the altar and its meaning, it seems to me that more and more our churches will become museum pieces—of the folk museum style—where the celebration of the Mass will seem utterly foreign.

The other problem that seems to me to have rather serious repercussions for the living faith of the churchgoer is the problem of funerals. In our parishes we have witnessed a proliferation of customs that are by and large shallow, the most far-fetched of these being the abandonment of black or violet in favor of other liturgical colors. Often, during the celebration of a funeral, one hears precious little more than Easter melodies. . . . Also, it is true that the hymns recommended for funeral masses are often quite deficient. . . .

But what strikes me as even more serious is the way certain practices are abandoned one after another on the pretext that they are merely a preparation for the way things are going to be in the Church of the future: for example, priests are pressured not to go to the cemetery anymore or else to go there in civilian dress. Practices of this kind can be justified, in a pinch, in the big cities, but in rural parishes they have absolutely no justification and are imposed from purely ideological considerations.

There is even worse news to report: the actual option of celebrating the Mass during a funeral is under siege. We are being encouraged to deny requests for a eucharistic celebration, and I know fellow pastors who think they have achieved a victory when they succeed in convincing a family that they should scratch the idea of a Mass of Christian burial.

In this respect, as well, a rediscovery of the meaning of the celebration of Christian death appears to me to be quite urgent, for if the Church is not present to lend significance to this tremendously important moment in life, who will take her place in doing so?

It seems to me . . . that the rite of Paul VI is in danger and that the preconciliar rite is making progress.

Whom should we blame? Certainly not the faithful of the "Tridentine" rite. For them their attachment to this rite is often a profound spiritual necessity. It is less and less a question of mere nostalgia. I know many young people who hold to this liturgy, even though their acquaintance with it is quite recent. Why is this so? Because there's nothing left, otherwise, but disorder, and the celebration of the rite of Paul VI—if it can still be called that—has been emptied of almost all its meaning. We should be happy that the faithful still have the chance to find a spiritual refuge in the Tridentine liturgy rather than losing their way—in certain places that I know of, that's the stage we've reached!

I know young people who, in following this path, have resumed the regular practice of their faith and have rediscovered their prayer life. Young people are still as sensitive to the serious side of life and a pursuit of the true and the beautiful. When this is rediscovered and acknowledged, our parish gatherings will be rejuvenated. . . .

Is this satisfactory? Not really, but I believe that when the rite of Paul VI rediscovers its true nature, the problem will no longer exist. But this is still far from being the case, for there are certain structural elements, on the practical level, that amount to stumbling blocks.

1. The idea of preparing the liturgy (rather than preparing for the liturgy): every parish wants to have its preparation team. The diocesan authorities encourage this. . . . What should be done? Things are disconnected and displaced. Innovations are eagerly sought out. Specialized journals are consulted. . . . "Laypeople need formation", it is said. All too true, but what kind of formation? And what kind of people should decide and direct the formation? Sometimes, moreover, the priest arranges to be absent during these preparations. . . .

2. The idea of participation: in itself, participation is a good thing, but it should be interiorized. In most of our churches, participation amounts to mere goose-stepping uniformity, useless discussions, doubtful innovations to promote the "participation" of the greatest number of people, a panoply of collages and posters. . . . All of this militates against true prayer and true participation in the Mystery.

3. The idea that things must be simplified (so as not to be "integralist"): the missal of Paul VI is rejected as such, and to apply it integrally is to be a "rubricist", to be lacking in "pastoral sense". . . . In this way much of the beauty and coherence of the liturgical act is lost. Recently I assisted at a procession with the Blessed Sacrament. I asked why there was no humeral veil. The answer I got was: "We've been given orders to keep things simple."

Unhappily, these three elements are so deeply rooted that, in my opinion, only the new generations of priests will be able to remedy them.

Finally, another point seems to me to require our attention: this is the whole issue of girl altar servers. An official text [1997] has appeared on this subject: this does not amount to an authorization, whatever some of the newspapers may have said about it. After that, there was a stampede . . . (as there had been already before). At a certain inter-parish meeting that I attended, it was proposed that the role of altar server be reserved solely for girls, who are better behaved. The pressure on priests is enormous—especially when the neighboring parish already has girls for the service of the altar. The whole thing is seen as an expression of the equality between boys and girls. The most tangible result is to drive away the boys or else to be left with only the very young boys.

And yet the "Instruction for the Ministry and Life of Priests" establishes a link between vocations to the priesthood and the service of the altar (to this line of argument I've had the following response: "But we also have to have vocations to the ranks of women religious").

What should a person do? . . . What steps should be taken?

FROM AN ABBOT

The question also arises why certain priests have ceased "to believe" in the liturgy and why the liturgy has ceased to please them!

What a storm has broken out among those members of the clergy who just can't manage—or are just plain disinclined—to look the Pope straight in the face and love their priesthood as it is, as they received it. . . . Oh how we need to pray! . . .

FROM A YOUNG LAYMAN

Allow me to contribute new testimony to the state and spirit of the liturgy that holds sway in some of our parishes in Île-de-France.

I was asked by a friend to help her prepare Sunday Mass. The two of us had a meeting with the organist and the person in charge of the singing as well as the celebrant. The first thing the celebrant did was ask us to drop the second reading (it was from the Letter of Saint Paul to the Thessalonians) on the pretext that it did not have any connection with the other two. . . . We had to bring a fair bit of sharp debate into the discussion in order to keep this second reading!

When we came to the penitential rite at the beginning of Mass, I suggested that the "I confess to Almighty God" should come before the "Lord Have Mercy". It was as if I had dropped a bomb. The whole tone of the meeting changed, as tensions mounted. I referred to the Roman Missal that I had brought with me, but the evidence of the official texts did nothing to win the case for me: no mere youth like myself, still wet behind the ears, was going to teach the presider of the celebration what he should be doing. The priest jumped up out of his chair, all hot under the collar. He wanted to leave and told me: "You won't force the 'I confess to Almighty God' on me!" At that point he made a straight-out threat not to celebrate Sunday Mass. We were forced to strike a compromise by resorting to another formula for the penitential rite: the third formula.

The priest accused me of "ritualism". All these preparatory discussions had to be done quite delicately, and that is why our *Gloria* was not right and the anamnesis was spoiled by the all too famous "Keep in mind that Jesus Christ".

This quarrel caused me real distress and deep sorrow: sincere collaboration is not possible, and what I have confirmed about this priest is true of his colleagues in our parish, even though some of them seem less rigid. What is the solution other than prayer on the one hand and flight on the other? Rather than arriving at mediocre compromises in a spirit of dissension, isn't it better to go elsewhere to see if God is there? Thus the rotten branches would be quicker to break off and tumble down. . . . Even at that you have to be able to find such an "elsewhere"! . . .

FROM A YOUNG LAYMAN

I should point out that it is no longer rare, in our town, to notice that the prayers at Sunday Mass are not those of the Roman Missal. For the most part, they are inspired by ideas proposed in certain journals, or else they are made up by the parish's liturgical team. Some of our priests have even put together their own "manual for celebration" containing several Eucharistic Prayers of their own making. . . . It goes without saying, of course, that these texts sometimes include passages that are not devoid of beauty or spiritual depth. This being so, it would be more correct, perhaps, for them to appear in works devoted to personal meditation or in collections designed for private prayer. But most often, apart from the fact that they

are not part of the liturgy of the Church (a quite sufficient reason to remove them from the celebration!), their
use during Sunday Masses reveals a tendency to excessive
wordiness and a kind of self-celebration on the part of the
congregation.

What is especially paradoxical about this dismissive attitude toward the official texts of the missal is the justification for it that is often put forward in good faith by many
of our priests: without the falsification of the Church's
liturgy being established in principle, it is maintained that
the invention of these prayers facilitates the participation
of the faithful, who thus take a greater interest in the celebration.

What is totally lost sight of, it seems, is that it is precisely the familiarity engendered by the ritual nature of
the liturgy that allows that "prayerful assimilation" that
is the basis of the "full, conscious, and active participation" required by *Sacrosanctum concilium*. So it is impossible not to mention the syntactic acrobatics or the
theological poverty occasioned by the Collects and Post-
Communion Prayers that are improvised by certain celebrants on a whim of the moment. When prayers like
this are compared with the splendidly rich prayers of the
missal of Paul VI, they retain hardly more than that little
end clause, "for ever and ever", which serves to strike
a chord with the faithful and plays with scant respect on
their purely reflexive reactions. The same feeling of regret
is inspired by the paraphrases of Saint-Exupéry and Khalil
Gibran voiced in certain homilies at nuptial Masses, when
the celebrant accedes to the couple's desire to read a text

that "speaks to them" or "meets them where they're at" instead of the epistle. . . .

For this reason numerous churches have witnessed the disappearance of that "uniformity of ritual and sentiment that is proper to the Catholic Church, the heir and continuator of the first Christian community, which was 'of one heart and soul'" (Acts 4:32), to use the words of Paul VI, when he introduced the restored Mass in the wake of the Council, also adding that "the unanimity of the Church's prayer is one of the signs and one of the strengths of her unity and her catholicity." Whereas Bishop Marini, the Pope's Master of Ceremonies, testifies to the benefits of the liturgical reform on a world scale and affirms that the Roman rite possesses "an equilibrium and a sobriety which allow it to adapt to all cultures", whereas this prelate believes that the reform that came after the Council favors its universal use in the Latin Church and thus sees "the possibility that it be adopted in all countries", numerous parishes in my diocese are going the other way, indulging in personalized celebrations that harm the unity desired by the Church.

. . . Despite this progressive disappearance of fidelity to liturgical unity, in the parish where I have been organist for ten years, we have been able to benefit from Sunday Masses that can be considered in keeping with the directives of the Church: respect for the missal and the lectionary, the wearing of the prescribed vestments, high-quality homilies explaining some particular aspect of Scripture, hymns chosen without any a priori hostility to the Gregorian tradition, times of silence during

Mass, the liturgical director eager only to help sing the hymns, and so on. It seems hardly necessary to add that, to my knowledge, no member of the faithful has ever complained about this approach or found himself "ill at ease".

Every Sunday, our pastor, who is an old man and, sadly, in poor health, would make use of photocopied sheets sent to him by the "pastoral sector" for the variable parts of the Mass. These sheets contained a short instruction for the beginning of Mass and well-written Prayers of the Faithful. Until the day when circumstances became such that our pastor asked me to write these introductions and Prayers of the Faithful myself. . . . Together with other people who were offering their services to help in the material preparation of the celebrations, we were able at that point to propose several improvements going in the direction of a better use of the riches to be found in the missal of Paul VI.

It was suggested, for example, that the "I confess to Almighty God" be recited more often instead of the brief formulas. It was proposed to reintroduce the rite of aspersion, which takes the place of penitential preparation, or also to use the solemn blessings provided for certain feasts. Also, the prayers were composed with the idea of adhering more faithfully to the indications given in the "General Instruction of the Roman Missal". In the same spirit, the use of a veil for the chalice (still obligatory) was reestablished, as was the use of a processional Cross —to the great delight of the altar boys. Also, the people who usually did the two readings before the Gospel decided that the introductory remarks for these two texts, which had been provided in the sheets that came from our "pastoral sector", were quite useless. They were abolished, since, according to the directives of the Church, they had no grounds for existing.

During the solemnity of the Assumption—despite the poor means that our parish has at its disposal (absence of a *schola*)—the presence of a friend . . . even allowed us to sing in its entirety *Kyriale VIII* . . . , which is no longer retained by any other church in our town.

In summary, many ideas were gathered together so that all the faithful of good will could sample the authentic prayer of the Church. The recent Council tells us that this prayer allows us to share in that heavenly liturgy which is celebrated in the holy city of Jerusalem toward which we journey as pilgrims.[1]

When our pastor had to leave, he was replaced by a "team" of priests who came to celebrate Sunday Mass in rotation. The situation underwent a rapid change. . . . Because of the merger of two parishes—including ours— the new pastor requested several people from our parish to go to a meeting with the "liturgical team" from the neighboring parish. According to our priest, everything went much more smoothly there than in our church, because the members of that "team" prepared the "layout of the celebrations" from week to week. They would compose a greeting for the congregation, a long introduction to be read at the microphone during the entrance of the celebrant, an "improved preface", certain parts of the Eucharistic Prayer intended to be proclaimed by those as-

---

[1] *Sacrosanctum concilium*, no. 8.

sisting at the Mass, and prayers intended to replace the presider's prayers given by the missal. . . . In short, the neighboring parish provided grist for the mill of those who oppose the liturgy restored by Vatican II, claiming that the so-called rite "of Paul VI" does not exist and that, as a result, they must hold fast to the Roman Missal of 1962 to be certain of having a stable liturgy that is doctrinally beyond reproach.

For this meeting of the two parishes to which I had been invited (and about whose orientation I had a sense of foreboding) I had brought the Acts of the Second Vatican Council, as well as *Vicesimus quintus annus*, the apostolic letter of December 4, 1988 . . . without any great illusions about the possibility of suggesting that some passages be read. In fact, even my carefully phrased remarks did not give me enough leverage to cite the official texts: our new pastor judged it useless to "return to those ancient texts" since "everything has evolved much farther since their time." Also, he gave all kinds of good reasons for urging us not to follow the liturgy of the Church, except that we, for our part, had to use the photocopied pages supplied by the "pastoral sector". Furthermore, they were all astonished that it was the youngest member of the gathering who had a mentality that was so "reactionary" as to ask that the Roman Missal should be respected: "How is this? You're only twenty-six, and you're stuck in this time warp?" I too could have expressed astonishment and asked the same thing of the oldest people present there: How was it that they were "stuck in a time warp", using terms and slogans that were being bandied about just after the Council about forty years ago?

At the end of the meeting, it was decided that our parish should subscribe to the journal *Signe d'aujourd'hui* (Bayard Editions). Then they went on to choose "themes of celebration" for each Sunday. As for the much-vaunted sheets put out by the "pastoral sector", this was what happened: with the utmost courtesy and calm I refused to photocopy them in our parish church.

The next day after this meeting, when I happened to meet our pastoral dean, I quickly explained the situation to him, trying not to come across as overbearing and taking care not to demand what I nonetheless considered an essential right. In an air of astonishment I no longer alluded to the documents of the Council or the Pope (for I knew that, according to our pastoral dean, "the Pope's way of celebrating Mass should not be considered a point of reference for the rest of the Church" [*sic*]) but rather to my personal reading: Jean Daujat, Dom Guy-Marie Oury. . . . Although he was quite good-natured about it, our dean responded that my reading was "slanted" and that, in any case, my remarks about the celebration of the Eucharist were not in accord with the thought and practice of our bishop.

Now it so happened that a seminarian friend of mine had just invited me to take part, that very same day, in a meeting with the bishop, who was making a pastoral visit to our town. . . .

That evening, our bishop had a brief conference on the Church and invited the people who were present with him to ask him questions. These dealt mostly with what the mass media have dubbed "the Gaillot affair". Therefore I took advantage of the disjointed nature of the meeting to approach the shepherd of our diocese and explain to him quite briefly the liturgical problems that I had just been confronted with. Without mentioning any names, I asked him quite simply what I should have replied to those who wanted to force me to print prayers that were foreign to those of the Roman Missal on sheets that were intended for use in the liturgy. Our bishop told me I was right to oppose practices like this, adding: "You have to understand quite clearly that these texts are not to be manipulated by anybody. Take heart!"

This is the reply that I communicated—courteously—to our pastor. Since that time we have continued to use the Roman Missal in our church for the celebration of Sunday Mass, except for the Sundays when, unhappily, the priest himself brings other texts. A few days later, I assisted at a Sunday Mass that was celebrated by our bishop. I noticed that he was presiding over the eucharistic celebration without a chasuble and reading the prayers on sheets that had been slipped into a plastic folder. The liturgy had been designed for the occasion by the priest who was organizing the get-together. Judging by the multicolored display panel that had been assembled for the meeting, blocking out the gothic choir of the church, we were quite far removed from the teaching given by the Pope in *Vicesimus quintus annus*, the letter he issued for the twenty-fifth anniversary of the Constitution on the Sacred Liturgy: celebrations at which the bishop presides "should be a model for the whole diocese". We were also far removed from the recommendations made during the European congress of liturgical officials, a congress whose acts have been recorded in the journal of the Congregation for Divine Worship and the Discipline of the Sacraments.

In comparison with these facts, I want merely to stress that the opinion proffered by the bishop of my diocese made some allowance at least for the wishes of anyone who did not want to be forced to act against the teaching of the Church—which is perfectly legitimate.

Nowadays, it is easy to see that the pervasive mentality is hardly receptive to the notions of obedience and fidelity to the Magisterium. The "anti-Roman affect", to use the famous expression coined by Hans Urs von Balthasar, "the destructive interpretation of pluralism", which prompted Paul VI's anxious exhortations during the 1970s, along with the weakening of the idea of thinking with the mind of the Church (i.e., *sentire cum ecclesia*) are indisputable realities that make the work of our Association on behalf of the liturgy difficult and yet necessary. The promotion of the authentic liturgy of the Church, both in its vernacular and Latin forms, is in keeping with the true reform that Cardinal Ratzinger desires for our time: "The *reformatio* that is necessary for our times does not consist in the notion that we should take it on ourselves at will to remodel and reinvent our Church indefinitely, but, quite to the contrary, in the notion that we should always be ready to clear away the debris in our own lives, so as to leave room for that pure light which comes from on high and which is also an inflowing of pure freedom."

From a Priest

Being neither an integralist nor a modernist, I have a great
thirst rather for an attitude of obedience to the Church,
which sees the liturgy as a divine reality. . . . In fact, however, a number of priests have transformed it into a matter
of whim and fancy. Laypeople have an inflated notion of
their own power, so that the priest finds himself having
the most absurdly fantastic liturgies imposed on him.

In January I had to do a funeral near a certain town.
It was impossible to find a chasuble. As for a thurible?
I was told that it's not something that's used anymore.
How many priests are there who offer only one gift at
the time of the Offertory and skip the washing of the
hands as well as the prayer after the Our Father (i.e.,
"Deliver us, Lord . . .")?

There was a funeral that took place at another town.
The person who was explaining the ceremony apologized
for the fact that there was Latin and Greek (without any
abuses, to be sure!) as if this were a concession to anti-
quated forms. . . . And what can be said about the hymns
that people choose? Quite often they smack of a horizontal stress on the "human" and are marked by a pathetic
poverty in terms of doctrine and aesthetics. In the case of
funerals, there is also the widespread practice of playing
the deceased person's favorite song at church. . . . These
are just a few examples. You would know of countless
others. As well, there is a dreadfully narrow sectarianism
on the part of certain laypeople and even priests with regard to others among the faithful, who are often scorned
and dismissed. They have no right to exist, it is said.

Appendix

FROM A BISHOP

There was a such a desire to change the way things were named that in the end serious realities were affected and authority was dissolved (under the pretext of providing services) to the benefit of parallel, clandestine authorities that are powerful and elusive. I cannot be emphatic enough in my denunciation of the harm that has been done to the Church in France by the councils, secretariats, and centers that have been established in Paris and enjoy sovereign rule over the pastoral situation in France. The members of these centers live together, they brainstorm frantically and sometimes vacuously, they coopt one another, and they have at their disposal offices, journals, newspapers, study sessions, and the opportunity to travel. And all this time the bishops, who are scattered geographically, do not know how to oppose these subtle, parallel authorities, or else they do not dare to. Even at Lourdes, many of the bishops do not dare to speak up, for they know that all around them there are journalists of every persuasion and representatives from all the centers in Paris. These will not scruple to pick up on their words and distort them and so give them bad press. A restoration of the personal and collective authority of the bishops is imperative, as is a diminution in the power of the national secretariats and centers. We also need to see numerous personnel changes, for there are many people who are out of place and have been coopted.

From a Laywoman

I went to a penitential celebration last April on the first of the month. There were about 150 people and six priests. No confessions but a general absolution even though we had the whole afternoon ahead of us. . . . As I was leaving the church, I remarked to one of the priests, "You didn't find that too tiring, I'm sure! I'm furious . . .", and then I left. We weren't even reminded that important sins had to be confessed. Even though people were still making the effort to come for confession when it came time for the Easter celebrations, there was nothing . . . not even contact with a priest. It was appalling.

From a Layman

I am writing to tell you that I was invited to the confirmation of one of my grand-nieces at the parish of Saint-Amand. In the church, the members of the congregation were seated and congratulating each another, while the young people hugged and kissed one another. . . . At the appointed time, the person who up to that point had been directing the choir as it rehearsed took the microphone to put an end to the commotion and introduced himself as the pastor of the parish. He told us that the ceremony would be presided over by a curate from the parish of St. Vincent de Paul assisted by his pastor.

The thirteen young people came forward, candle in hand, and went to stand in front of the altar. There, each one of them read from a sheet of paper on which he had written his "witness story" . . . , the reading of each of these accounts being punctuated by an entrance song that the curate accompanied on his guitar. . . .

Since this was vocation Sunday, the curate made sure he mentioned the bishops' meeting, which was concerned with pastoral approaches to young people. Indeed, from a presentation that had been made to the bishops on cassette the curate lifted the following phrase, quoting it to the whole congregation: "Rome smells of mothballs and needs a cleaning."

At the Offertory, the thirteen young people brought up "plates" containing hosts, as well as pitchers of water and wine. A ceramic goblet served as a ciborium.

At the Our Father we had to make a chain by holding hands. Although I was beside my nephew, I held my missal with both hands, as I consider the Our Father first and foremost to be a vertical prayer, not a horizontal one. But soon after that the concelebrating pastor invited the congregation to give one another the sign of peace. This meant that the thirteen young people had to leave the sacred space they had been occupying around the altar in order to spread out through the whole church.

FROM A YOUNG PRIEST

I am a young priest, aged thirty, and I consider that the liturgy, when it is celebrated with dignity, can become the foremost means to achieve a deepening of our faith.

. . . I would like to share with you my reflections on one particular element of the liturgy, specifically, "liturgical floral arrangement". This is an aspect that may seem quite secondary, although in my opinion it shows to what degree a poor understanding of the liturgy can reach the heights of absurdity. To give you an example of what is happening more and more, I shall refer you to a parish where, a short while ago, an armada of dedicated people took care of the cleaning and decoration of the church, a historical monument of great size. Everything was going well until, one day, one of them, having taken courses in the art of liturgical floral arrangement, proclaimed that she was the only one entitled to decorate the sacred space. What had she learned in these courses? That simple bouquets had to be abandoned in favor of more or less complex "compositions" whose merit is grandly supposed to be nothing less than "to present the meaning of the liturgy". That's why during Advent an old tree trunk is set down before the altar to signify a time of waiting . . . (?) During Lent, the priest says Mass in front of a heap of sand and pebbles, which are supposed to represent the desert . . . (one shudders to think what sort of "liturgical composition" they would come up with for the Sunday that features the Gospel passage about Jesus calming the storm . . .). Sometimes the priest has to make sure he doesn't step on a bouquet (although the question is whether three rocks with a single flower in the middle can still be called a bouquet) that is meant to represent humility. . . . Sometimes even the lighting is adjusted to blend with these esoteric works. Nowadays all this kind of thing is encouraged by "liturgical journals" in which the seriousness and pretension of the explanations cannot hide the absurdity of the whole process.

In the face of this crackpot fad that is invading our churches little by little, I ask myself: What is being made fun of? Is it not plain to see that hidden behind the inanities of this pop theology is the shapeless mysticism of the New Age movement?

From a Young Priest

It has been my observation as well that it is easier today, in France, to get a Mass celebrated according to the "Tridentine rite" than a Mass "of Paul VI" celebrated in accordance with the rules.

For my part, I see two main reasons of unequal weight that account for this situation.

1. It is easier to give permission to a voluntary group than to reform the clergy as a whole. This brings us to one of the essential elements of the crisis that the church in our country is undergoing: the clergy. The clergy is the main culprit (as it has been each time there have been serious crises). Question: What is being done to improve the formation of the clergy in terms of the liturgy, for one thing? This leads us in turn to question the value of certain documents that serve to "help" priests (Saint Brieuc sheets, the journal *Signe*, etc.).

2. One often hears it said jokingly about some liturgical change that is thought to be unimportant: "They're changing our religion." Let me ask the question: What if this were true? *Lex orandi, lex credendi.* Haven't the violent, anarchic changes that have occurred for the last thirty years changed the beliefs of the faithful and a great

many of the clergy? Alas, it is my strong fear that a question like this must be answered in the affirmative.

We find that altars have been turned around and replaced (in the best-case scenario) with less expensive tables, that sacred vessels have been replaced with earthenware, that liturgical vestments have been discarded, that socio-political chit-chat has been ensconced at the heart of the celebration. . . . All these things have served to abolish any notion of sacrifice in favor of an outlook that is solely preoccupied with the idea of a communal celebration or get-together. I take as an example what strikes me as very serious: for many years, I have noticed, during the summer, but also at certain gatherings, that an ever greater number of priests, dressed in civilian clothes, have been ''concelebrating'' with the congregation and receiving only the Body of Christ in Communion. I have queried some of them, but clearly they do not understand why they should be receiving the Precious Blood at Communion as well, since the principal celebrant has already done so. In their minds, Communion is merely a way to express participation in a communal action.

Also, if one looks at the manner in which many of our celebrations take place, the question that springs to mind is: Where is the respect that is owed to the Eucharist? It is not, by and large, to be found at Communion time. . . .

Given these conditions, how can priests and Christian communities be asked to have a dignified celebration in a rite whose meaning and intent they no longer understand, when, that is, they do not reject it outright?

I believe that the real rejection of the liturgy ''of Paul VI'' can be found—for reasons of faith—among those who vaunt themselves as the greatest defenders of "the spirit of the Council". This leads us as well to questions about the formation of priests and laypeople.

Also, I have noticed that many priests who have been sent for further studies so that they might, in turn, teach formation programs have big problems with their faith. They do their advanced studies, but they lack a feel for their subject matter.

This is easily explainable if one considers that they have been "selected" by persons who have the same difficulties. This raises the question of how those who do the formation are chosen and coopted.

I hope I have not been too negative, but I am one of those people who think that for an abscess to be healed it has to be lanced and that for evil to be overcome there should always be an attempt made to seek out its source.

FROM A FRENCH BISHOP

To my knowledge, there is no need for special permission to celebrate the Mass "of Paul VI" in Latin. I, for my part, regret that in actual fact it is never celebrated, even at international gatherings, and I also regret that those who like Latin are most often of the opinion that only the "Tridentine" Mass can be celebrated in Latin. I regret even more keenly still that those who do not like Latin think that the mere fact of singing the *Gloria* or the *Credo*, let alone the celebration of the Mass "of Paul VI" in Latin, is a sign of integralism and disloyalty to Vatican II. . . .

. . . I can only applaud the initiative you have undertaken[2] not to let it be forgotten that the missal of Paul VI, in its original edition, is in Latin and that it was never intended that the versions of it in "vernacular" languages should serve to abolish this original edition.

---

[2] What is being referred to here is the *Pro Liturgia* Association—ED.

Bibliography

Works Consulted

Barthe, C. *Trouvera-t-il encore la foi sur terre? Une crise de l'Église: Histoire et questions.* Paris: F. X. de Guibert, 1996.

Bonnet, G. *Célébrer en vérité: Pratique religieuse et tâches humaines.* Paris: Centurion, 1983.

Bourdarias, J. *Les Évêques de France et le marxisme.* Paris: Fayard, 1990.

Catalan, J.-F. *Expérience spirituelle et psychologie.* Paris: Desclée de Brouwer, 1991.

———. *L'Homme et sa religion: Approche psychologique.* Paris: Desclée de Brouwer, 1993.

Chalmel, P. *Écône ou Rome: Le Choix de Pierre.* Paris: Fayard, 1990.

Congrégation pour le Clergé. *Directoire pour le ministère et la vie des prêtres.* Vatican, 1994.

Dem, M. *Évêques français, qu'avez-vous fait du catéchisme?* Paris: La Table Ronde, 1984.

Dreyfus, F. G. *Des évêques contre le pape.* Paris: Grasset, 1985.

Favreau, F. *La Liturgie.* Paris: Desclée, 1983.

Frossard, A. *Le Parti de Dieu: Lettre ouverte aux évêques.* Paris: Fayard, 1992.

Gleason, R., and G. Hagmaier. *Direction, éducation et psychopathologie*. Paris: Aubier Montaigne, 1962.

Hanotel, V. *Les Cathos*. Paris: Plon, 1995.

John Paul II. "On the Mystery and Worship of the Eucharist, *Dominicae Cenae*, February 24, 1980". Boston: Daughters of St. Paul, 1980.

———. *Vicesimus quintus annus* (December 4, 1988). In *The Pope Speaks* 34 (September-October 1989): 221–32.

Le Gall, R. *La Messe au fil des ses rites*. Tours: C.L.D., 1992.

La Liturgie, trésor de l'Église. Paris: C.I.E.L., 1995.

Manaranche, A. *Vouloir et former des prêtres*. Paris: Fayard, 1994.

Pour célébrer la messe. Tours: C.L.D., 1989.

Ratzinger, Joseph. *Feast of Faith*. Translated by Graham Harrison. San Francisco: Ignatius Press, 1986.

———. *A New Song for the Lord: Faith in Christ and Liturgy Today*. New York: Crossroad, 1996.

Ratzinger, J., and Vittorio Messori. *The Ratzinger Report: An Exclusive Interview on the State of the Church*. Translated by Salvator Attanasio and Graham Harrison. San Francisco: Ignatius Press, 1985.

Sacred Congregation for the Sacraments and Divine Worship. "Instruction Concerning Worship of the Eucharistic Mystery, *Inaestimabile Donum*, April 17, 1980." Boston: Daughters of St. Paul, 1980.

Soulages, G. *Épreuves chrétiennes et espérance*. Paris: Téqui, 1979.

Vandeur, E. *La Sainte Messe: Notes sur sa liturgie*. Namur: Abbaye de Maredsous, 1946.

Various Publications

Esprit et Vie. Weekly. Langres.

Notitiae. Official bulletin of the Congregation for Divine Worship. Vatican Editions.

Enchiridion Documentorum Instaurationis Liturgicae. Vatican Editions.

Documents of Vatican II.

Roman Missal. Vatican edition of 1962 and current Vatican edition of 1975 (Latin versions).

Caeremoniale episcoporum. Vatican Editions, 1985.

Pro Liturgia. Monthly Bulletin of the Association for the Promotion of the Roman Liturgy in Latin.[1]

Una Voce. Bimonthly Bulletin of the Association for the Preservation and Promotion of the Latin Liturgy, Gregorian Chant, and Sacred Art within the Roman Catholic Church.[2]

---

[1] The *Pro Liturgia* Association works for the faithful application of all the principles of the Council, so that the current liturgy, no longer subject to arbitrary manipulation, may blossom forth in dignity and beauty both in its vernacular form as well as its Latin, Gregorian form.

[2] Unlike the *Pro Liturgia* Association, the *Una Voce* Association (Paris, France) is asking for a return to the liturgy that was in use before the Second Vatican Council.